AMSTERDAM BY NIGHT

Frommer's

AMSTERDAM
by Night

BY

LAURA KELLY

A BALLIETT & FITZGERALD BOOK

MACMILLAN • USA

a disclaimer

Prices fluctuate in the course of time, and travel information changes under the impact of the varied and volatile factors that influence the travel industry. Neither the author nor the publisher can be held responsible for the experiences of readers while traveling. Readers are invited to write to the publisher with ideas, comments, and suggestions for future editions.

about the author

Laura Kelly has worked as a newpaper reporter, a magazine editor, a radio talk show host, a travel writer, and an essayist, and currently teaches journalism at Florida International University in Miami.

Balliett & Fitzgerald, Inc.
Executive editor: Tom Dyja
Managing editor: Duncan Bock
Associate editor: Howard Slatkin
Assistant editor: Maria Fernandez
Editorial assistant: Ruth Ro, Bindu Poulose

Macmillan Travel art director: Michele Laseau

All maps © Simon & Schuster, Inc.

MACMILLAN TRAVEL
A Simon & Schuster Macmillan Company
1633 Broadway
New York, NY 10019

ISBN 0-02-861137-3
Library of Congress information available from Library of Congress.

special sales

Bulk purchases (10+ copies) of Frommer's and selected Macmillan travel guides are available to corporations, organizations, institutions, and charities at special discounts, and can be customized to suit individual needs. For more information write to Special Sales, Macmillan General Reference, 1633 Broadway, New York, NY 10019.

Manufactured in the United States of America

contents

Central Amsterdam Orientation

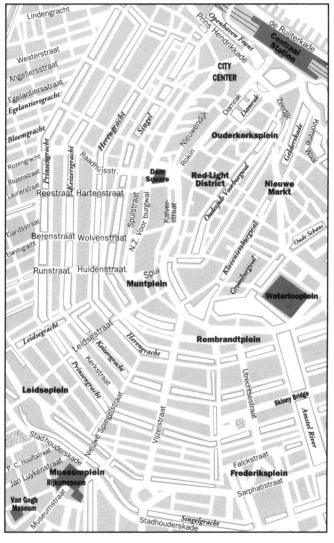

Museumplein Area &
Amsterdam South Orientation

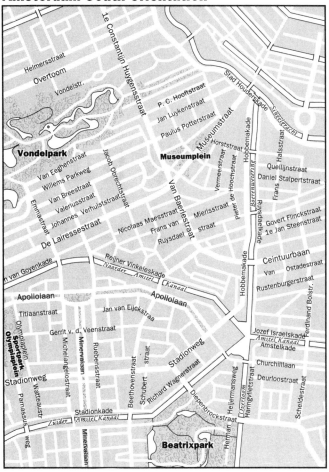

what's
hot,
what's
not

If Paris is high heels, Amsterdam is Hush Puppies. The Dutch are no backwater rubes; they just simply can't be bothered with policing fashion or fretting over codes of the cool. It has to do with the national cult of *gezelligheid*—a term with no English equivalent that refers to everything from a lived-in, cozy neighborhood cafe to a really great experience. Don't worry about it. Just go with it. In the Dutch psyche, the interior always takes precedence over the exterior (in Amsterdam feeling marvelous is much preferred to looking marvelous). It's a laissez faire town. At night, blue jeans, bikes (as in pedals, not Harleys), and beer are the Holy Trinity. So here's what you *won't* need in this relentlessly casual city: no car, no designer clothes, no big-budget wad of cash, no attitude.

Instead, bring a heart. Don't be a robot. Amsterdam may be famous as a modern Sodom, but we say skip the Red Light Distrtict and the smoking coffeeshops (actually, you *need* to be high to enjoy the RLD's ridiculous tourist-trap stage shows). The real Amsterdam is far richer. It's a city of jazz, opera, cozy neighborhood hangouts known as brown cafes, theater, and streetlife. You can hear free live music every night of the week in small, smoky clubs and in public squares. Jazz is Amsterdam's heartbeat, the soundtrack for a town more interested in soul than show. The culture-vulture in us all can witness cutting edge modern dance and movement theater: Dutch audiences clamor for innovation, making the stage scene one of Europe's most exciting. Or for a night of hypnotic party music, check out the sound that Dutch clubbers have made their own: trance and the Indian-inflected goa trance music. It's like mind syrup. Or you can ponder anarchist art in squatted performance spaces. Or peck at a *rijsttafel*, a smorgasbord of Indonesian food that has become Amsterdam's adopted local cuisine. Go local and go slowly: Spend the night sampling beer in a brown cafe, jousting over politics, and savoring the lights of the city reflecting off the canals. Amsterdam's allure is free for everyone—and there's practically no dress code. Experiment. Revel. And then try to remember the name of your hotel.

What's hot

Opera on Tuesdays... Of all the city's classical arts, opera has become *the* rage in Amsterdam. Why? The Dutch never had a Grand Opera tradition like the Italians, or even the English; and at the **Muziektheater** (see The Arts), a daring artistic director has swept away the cobwebs of the 19th century's favorite medium. Instead of big-time opera names on the Stopera (as it's locally known) marquee, productions are quirky and inventive: singers with pink hair, minimal orchestration, unusual collaborations, theater and music stars making guest appearances. The results have drawn younger crowds that would be just as likely to show up at a David Byrne concert or an Eric Bogosian monologue. The good news: Amsterdam opera tickets are some of the cheapest in Europe; good seats go for less than Dfl 100. And the Dutch, a nations of traders at heart, know a good deal when they see one; so expect packed houses on the cut-rate weeknight performances. Go with the backpackers, starving artists, and economically challenged. Opera on Tuesday is not just a bargain, it's a scene.

Techno and trance... The Dutch band in the forefront of American musical memory is most likely Golden Earring, who hit the seventies pop charts with their irritating single "Radar Love." But the times, they are a-changing. Rock and roll is not where it's at in Amsterdam clubs (or on the airwaves). The Dutch instead have begun exporting alternative music. Channel surf onto MTV and you'll spot 2 Unlimited, with their techno dance tracks, or the metalheads Gorefest. But the hottest export of all may be trance music. It's like Jean-Michel Jarre's New Age easy-listening remade for happy-go-lucky clubbers. Walls of synthesized, moody sound purr from club speakers, laced with driving-but-never-distracting back beats. Hot bands like trance musicmeisters Quazar or Germanating Seeds of Doda, who make goa trance, can be heard at clubs like **Red** or **Amnesia** (see The Club Scene).

Amsterdam Arena... When it opened in August 1996, the arena incited the local press to trot out a grab bag of adjectives like state-of-the-art, high-tech, cutting edge, and futuristic. The Arena has also invited comparisons to a Big Mac, a UFO and a concrete bathtub. With an eerie resemblance to the spacecraft in *Close Encounters of the Third Kind*, the silver, domed arena dominates the city's southeastern skyline. The 150,000-seat stadium is the home base for the soccer team **Amsterdam Ajax** (see

Sports) and hosts rock concerts, operas, conventions, exhibitions, and conferences. The arena's design—including a sliding roof to keep inclement weather at bay and a highway that runs beneath the structure—has drawn worldwide attention, including visits from the Aussies who will host the Olympics in 2000 and the French who are constructing a stadium for the World Cup 1998.

Summer sunlight... And we're not talking temperature. Henry James called Amsterdam "perfect prose." He must have been visiting between May and September when the sun doesn't set until 10pm, which means you can get daylight in your nightlife.

Safe sex... The ongoing, provocative, progressive, and highly visible ad campaign to encourage safe sex and condom use is papered all over Amsterdam on bus and tram stops, billboards, and free postcards distributed in restaurants and clubs. Seductively good looking mixed-gender and same-sex couples in various stages of pre-coital undress hold little, cellophane-wrapped squares under the banner headline, "Your condom or mine?" The tag line at the bottom reads, *Ik vrij veilig of ik vrij niet* ("I make safe love or I don't make love"). The campaign is indicative of the Dutch government's liberal attitude toward AIDS awareness and education.

Columbus... Columbus is a wheat beer that's all the rage in a city famous for Heineken, Amstel, Grolsch, and Oranjeboom. Brewed locally in the Bierbrouwerij t' IJ, a microbrewery in a windmill, the reddish beer is powerful (almost 10 percent alcohol content), hearty, and full flavored. "It's beer you can chew," one local quipped. You'll find it in bars and restaurants around the city, like **Cafe de Wildeman** or **Nota Bene** (see The Bar and Cafe Scene).

Bad TV... A zany Dutch television show called *Over de Rooien* airs on SBS6 three nights a week at 6:30pm, which is just about the time people are in their hotel rooms dressing to go out for the evening. The name translates into "out of their minds" and the show is a kamikaze mix of "Candid Camera," "Gong Show," "American Gladiators," and "That's Incredible." Even if you can't speak a word of Dutch, the program is mostly sight gags that speak the international language of outrageous stupidity. Two hosts roam the streets of Amsterdam with a camera crew and offer passersby a 1000 guilder note to be silly on camera. A few of their challenges: Paint your name on a poster board with your hair as a paintbrush and have one of the first three people you stop on the sidewalk be able to read it. Approach strangers and ask them if you can cut off their neckties and collect a dozen within 10 minutes. Within 15 minutes, find a woman who will expose her breasts on camera. To fully appreciate the show, keep in mind that while this sort of public silliness is *de rigeur* for Americans, the Dutch are much more circumspect and private.

What's not

Government support for the arts... For a cushy 40 years from the end of World War II until the end of the eighties, the Dutch government provided beefy subsidies for the arts and its creators, which kept artists off the streets and earned the country the status as one of the a small handful of European countries that actively (read: financially) supported the arts. As the Netherlands, like many of its European brethren, has begun choking on the high costs of benevolent government, an unfortunate austerity has replaced largesse, and the nineties have meant leaner budgets and reshuffled governmental priorities. The process of weaning the arts from state funding has yielded less experimentation and fewer fringe arts groups—two of the most exciting elements of the Dutch arts scene. Even mainstream arts groups such as the Netherlands Philharmonic have scrambled for corporate and foundation sponsorship. Some museums have jacked up admission prices (the Rijksmusuem, for example), and others that were once free (the Verzetsmuseum) have introduced entry fees. (See The Arts.)

Magnanimity... The Dutch pride themselves on their *zuinigheid*, which means thriftiness. It's admirable enough until you're on the receiving end. Case in point: The Dutch custom of serving beer. The tap is pulled; a head foams onto the top, and instead of letting the bubbles settle and filling the actual liquid to the top of the glass, the Dutch swath the top of the beer with a plastic spatula and serve it with a foam head the width of two fingers. By the time the foam recedes, you're left with a glass of beer that looks like your neighbor took two sips while you weren't looking.

Athletic footwear... Though Amsterdam is a sophisticated urban center, it is refreshingly lax on its fashion rules. Slouchy, industrio-urban wear from the Gap or Benneton or Banana Republic dominate the runways that are the city streets, unlike Paris where locals sniff at anything that doesn't have chic. The only unbreakable fashion no no at play in Amsterdam: sports shoes as night time footwear. Nikes at night? Just *don't* do it. Bouncers at clubs will give you the thumbs down and locals will immediately peg you as the hapless tourist you are showing yourself to be.

Late night dining... Unlike Madrid, Athens, Rome, Miami, or Paris, Amsterdam is not a city where eating out begins at 11pm. The custom of earlier dining—say by 8 or 9pm—doesn't bespeak a lack of sophistication, it's merely the Dutch way. In Amsterdam, eating out is not usually the centerpiece of the night, it's an early evening pit stop, a prelude to hitting the clubs, catching a movie, attending the ballet, cafe hopping. It is possible to forage for food in the later hours of the evening (this is a big city, after all), but choices are severely limited. Most of the city's restaurants close their kitchens by 11pm and shut their doors at midnight. (See Late Night Dining.)

the clu

b scene

1

From aural sax to oral sex,
Amsterdam's club scene
proffers the hedonistic
trinity of sex, drugs, and
music with evangelical zeal.
The sex is for sale within
the carnal realm of the

Red Light District. The drugs are parceled out in herbal packets from smoking coffeeshops. And the music is everywhere in the city's jumping club scene. Live music is one of Amsterdam's main food groups. From cavernous clubs that hold hundreds of gyrating groovesters to dim, smoky spaces no larger than a living room, it is possible to hear live music, and especially jazz, every night of the week. The club music—both live and canned—reads like an all-you-can-eat menu: acid jazz, Dixieland jazz, fusion jazz, trance, goa-trance, techno, trip-hop, hip hop, house, rock and roll, rap, experimental space music, high nrg, subsonic future funk, salsa, ska, soul, grunge, punk, disco, funkyjunglehiphopdub, swing, world, and folk.

Amsterdam is on the map as a jazz city; you'll hear all styles played in small cafes like **Bamboo Bar** and in the legendary **Bimhuis**, the city's premiere jazz club, where Miles, Bird, Coltrane and all the illuminati have performed. Local jazz names to look for include saxophonists Hans Dulfer (the so-called father of Amsterdam jazz holds court every Wednesday night at the small, smoky **Alto Jazz Café**), Bill Breuker, and percussionist Martin van Duyhoven.

One of the things differentiating this city's clublife from that of other sophisticated urban centers is the surprising dearth of attitude, gouging entry fees, and fashion-policing. Cover charges usually run no more than Dfl 10, and plenty of clubs charge nada for live tunes, including Alto Jazz Café, **Canaçao Rio**, **Café Meander**, and **Korsakoff**. Clubs with a dress code—**RoXy**, **Richter**, **Naar Boven**, **Escape**, **Sinners in Heaven**—are more fashion lax than in chic cities like New York, Paris, or London. Generally verboten are running shoes and shorts and anything overtly dorky, but you don't need designer anything to pass muster in this city. The word is casual.

Theme nights are the current rage, sort of a Sybil approach some clubs take to showcasing their multiple personalities. Monday night might be British pop disco, Tuesdays trance, Wednesdays surf tunes and beachwear. Thursdays would then be ceded to subsonic future funk and assorted trippy tunes, Fridays to gay disco raves, and on Saturdays house tunes would thump out the week. The guide, the Bible, the compass to clubs and themes and parties and bands is the free, weekly English glossy leaflet called *To The Point*. Piles of them are stacked in clubs, restaurants, bookstores, hotels.

Etiquette

Because Amsterdam is compact and highly walkable, a night of clubbing usually means visiting three or four places. Doors open at about 11pm, critical mass is reached by about 3am, and last call isn't yelled until 5am.

Two local club customs to abide: You must pay for toilets. A bathroom attendant prowls the loo area and expects at least 50 cents usually clinked into a saucer. If you leave the club and expect to return, local etiquette requires that you tip the doorman at least a guilder or two.

Central Amsterdam Clubs

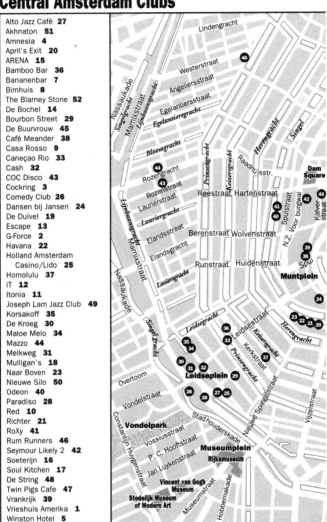

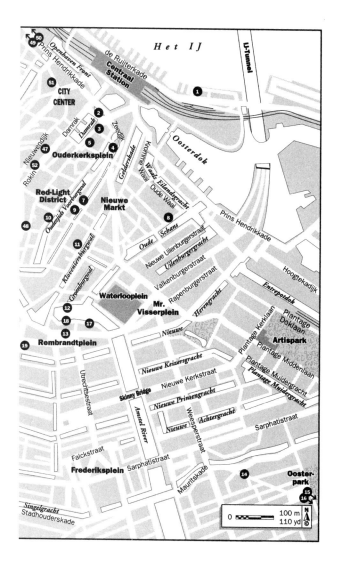

Het IJ

de Ruijterkade

Openhaven Front
Prins Hendrikkade

Centraal Station

IJ-Tunnel

51 CITY CENTER

2

Damrak

Zeedijk

3

5

Nieuwendijk

47

Damrak

4

Ouderkerksplein

Gelderskade

52

Rokin

Kromme Waal

Oude Waal

Oosterdok

Waals Eilandsgracht

Red-Light District

7

Nieuwe Markt

Oudezijds Voorburgwal

9

8

10

48

Prins Hendrikkade

11

Oude Schans

Nieuwe Uilenburgerstraat

Uilenburgergracht

Uilenburgerstraat

Valkenburgerstraat

Rapenburgerstraat

Klaveniersburgwal

Groenburgwal

Hoogtekadijk

Entrepotdok

Waterlooplein

Herengracht

Mr. Visserplein

12

18

17

13

Rembrandtplein

19

Plantage Kerklaan

Plantage Doklaan

Artispark

Nieuwe

Plantage Middenlaan

Plantage Muidergracht

Nieuwe Keizersgracht

Plantage Muidergracht

Utrechtsestraat

Nieuwe Kerkstraat

Skinny Bridge

Nieuwe Prinsengracht

Amstel River

Nieuwe Achtergracht

Weesperstraat

Sarphatistraat

Falckstraat

Frederiksplein

Sarphatistraat

Mauritskade

14

Ooster-park

15

16

Singelgracht

Stadhouderskade

0 — 100 m
— 110 yd

N

Clubs in the Museumplein Area & Amsterdam South

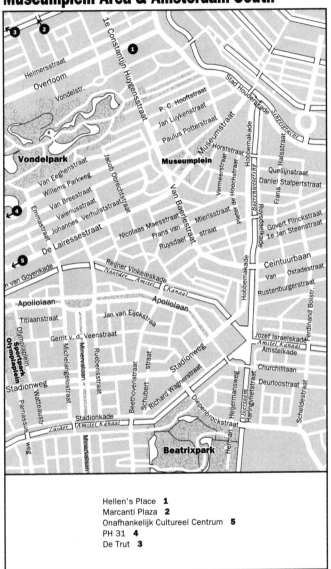

Hellen's Place **1**
Marcanti Plaza **2**
Onafhankelijk Cultureel Centrum **5**
PH 31 **4**
De Trut **3**

All that jazz... Amsterdam has a fat menu of venues for anyone jonesing to hear jazz. Every July, Holland is the worldwide jazz mecca in the guise of the North Sea Jazz Festival in the Hague, a short train ride from Amsterdam. More than 700 musicians flock here for three non-stop days of jazz on a dozen stages. During October, smaller jazz festivals are held around Amsterdam. All year round, weekend jazz brunches are popular at designer cafes like the baroque **Du Lac** (see The Bar and Cafe Scene), and during the summer, centrally located Vondelpark and other al fresco venues and parks sponsor jazz concerts.

After sundown, a broad menu of jazz choices begins with **Bimhuis** (locals chop the name in half and call it *Bim*), the acknowledged ringleader of Amsterdam's jazz clubs and the spot local jazz aficionados acknowledge as Mecca. Big-name jazz performers have shows here on weekends; weeknights, local talent congregates for free jam sessions. Some local music fans and jazz zealots say the Bim lost a bit of its soul when it renovated several years ago to expand into what is now an auditorium and a bar. Gone is the raffishness, the frayed charm one yearns for where saxophones play, but the stellar quality of the jazz remains. On a street off Leideseplein, **Alto Jazz Café** announces its purpose with a two-story sax affixed to its facade. Inside, it's Central Casting jazz cafe: smoky, cramped, beguilingly offbeat. Dollars, lire, francs, marks, and yen form makeshift wallpaper behind the bar. Dented trumpets hang from the ceiling; posters from the North Sea Jazz Festival have a yellow patina from clouds of cigarette smoke. Wearing thick collars of wax, candles flicker from the dark wooden bartop. Live jazz is performed here nightly—no cover, but the place is small and fills fast. On Wednesdays, don't miss the local sax legend Hans

Dulfer. If the **Alto** is sardined, in the same 'hood is the tiki tiki **Bamboo Bar**, another small club with a crammed-in stage and no dance floor to speak of. Nightly free music is offered here and ranges from jazz to rock to world. At **Bourbon Street**, the jazz tilts toward the sort that is usually preceded by the words "good-time", namely Dixieland and parade jazz. More mainstream than its brethren, this club attracts a beatnik-free crowd more comfortable with Marvin Hamlisch than Miles Davis. Dixieland alternates with traditional 1950s jazz standards (read: jazz lite) at the **Joseph Lam Jazz Club** in the Scheepvart district west of Centraal Station. This place seems firmly entrenched as couples' territory on Saturday nights; the free Sunday jam sessions lure a younger audience hoping for some fusion or acid jazz riffs.

Toughest to get into... *Hipness maximus* is the mantra at the dance club **RoXy** (an acronym for Radical Outlet for the Xenomaniac in You), the see-and-be-seen apex of heterosexual Amsterdam nightlife. Part of the lure to the multilevel, bacchanalian venue is the megabucks sound system reverberating house, trip hop, and garage tunes. Amsterdam's glitterati party here—Ajax soccer stars, Euro groovesters, visiting musicians and actors, and the attendant covey of glamorous specimens. Theme nights offer a smorgasbord approach. The Sunday night Pussy Lounge attracts lipstick lesbians, Wednesdays are gay nights with buff boys by the dozens, and monthly New Age nights lure life's mellow, bearded, and sandaled subcultures. Officially a members-only club, the unstated door policy can be daunting (being beautiful, wearing black, and feigning ennui always helps). Thursday nights (when the door policy seems its most lax) features guest deejays like white-hot Dimitri and Franki D., who spins subsonic future funk (think "The Jetsons" meets Rick James meets Thomas Dolby).

Humbled by the fickle nature of nowness, Thursday or Sunday night at **Sinners in Heaven** may look like a morgue. On Fridays after midnight, however, lines of clubbers hoping to pass fashion and aura muster snake around the block, awaiting the nod and the entrée into the pleasure dome. Inside, the decor lurches toward Vegas in high velocity, with dry ice commingling with cigarette smoke, revolving disco balls, and endless other reflective surfaces. Cavernous as an airplane hangar, **Escape** is a seventies-redux meat market at home in the honky tonk, neon blare of Rembrandtplein. Only a happening thing on weekends, Escape is zealously guarded by beefy bouncers with Billy Ray Cyrus haircuts and the caprice of spoiled rich kids. Dress for excess is the code here, and be prepared to cajole for entry. There is room for 2,000 people, most of whom gravitate toward tight skirts and bilevel poodle hair or gold chains and shirts unbuttoned to reveal throw rugs of chest hair, all invoking the eerie feeling that you've tripped back in time and landed on the set of *Saturday Night Fever.* Occasional live acts perform here—Naughty By Nature, Exposé—and other nights are ceded to the usual bag of tricks: thumping disco, and manic, colored lights slicing through the darkness.

Not worth getting into... The inside joke of retro 1970s decor has been lost on **Cash,** a little nightclub just off Leidseplein that looks as if it has always preferred polyester and shag carpets. Plastic palm trees wag from the corner of the place, which may have added its small dance floor as an afterthought. Low ceilings, chrome detailing, and wretched Top 40 music complete the dismal scenario. Someone pull the plug.

The only thing worse than a small nightclub that just can't achieve liftoff is a large nightclub grappling with the same predicament. **Marcanti Plaza** is one of the city's largest clubs—it holds 3,000—but the soulless venue has never captured the attention of the city's trendsetters. This is teeny-bopper central, larval white trash. The club is suffused with an air of desperation and a clientele that look as if they live in the same neighborhood as Roseanne's TV character (they may; this club is a heavy fave of 'burb dwellers from provincial Holland). They're doing the White Man's Overbite when they boogey down at **Lido,** the downstairs club at the Holland Amsterdam Casino. Upstairs is the casino, somewhere between Vegas and Atlantic City on the food chain. Downstairs, the Lido is a cabaret-*cum*-dinner club-*cum*-dance floor in equally cheesy doses. Decorated in no-risk glitz like a Holiday Inn lounge going to the prom, this place pulls in flocks of tourist buses and entertains the vanilla hordes they disgorge.

THE CLUB SCENE ◟ THE LOWDOWN

Where the big names play... A mainstay on the Amsterdam nightlife scene for at least two decades, the venerable **Melkweg** has mushroomed from a former dairy into a full-fledged entertainment center, with an art gallery, a bar/restaurant, a video room, a theater, a cinema, a tea room, and two halls featuring live bands. It's a cavernous, user-friendly place with no dress code, attitude, or predominant age group. Just off the neon nocturne of Leideseplein, it draws consistently thick crowds for the big-name rockers that play here (Sonic Youth, Phish, Cranberries) and for the everchanging theme nights (the latest sampler: Beatlemania, Surf's Up, Techno Future Noize Tunes), host DJs spin an aural menu ranging from hip hop to house to ska. A short stroll away is **Paradiso**, housed in a converted 17th-century church and another major-player club that doubles as a venue for visiting A-team bands. Inside, a huge balcony encircles the interior and affords ace views of the main dance floor/stage below. Ceilings are majestically high, enriching the acoustics and the atmosphere. Visiting musical acts range from homegrown talent to Joan Osborne; theme nights (the rage in this city) include raves, Jazz Bop parties, and Britpop disco.

Hip hop and punk on the turntable... In a city dominated by trance-inducing, high-tech dance music, DJs who spin good ol' U.S. rabblerousers like hip hop and punk can be hard to find. But there is some hope. At **Korsakoff** on Lijnbaansgracht, mannequins hang horizontally from the ceiling, suspended by chains. Orange walls sallow the complexion of the rasty green-haired 18-year olds with tie-dyed T-shirts circling small tables just off the dance floor. Punk and grunge are the favored tracks, and you get the feeling the bored, blue-jeaned patrons want to mosh until dawn. Drinks are cheap, entry is free, and local bands perform live on weekends. Puzzlingly bereft of a club that plays hip hop regularly, Amsterdam's clubs (**Akhnaton**, **Melkweg**, **Seymour Likely 2**) instead sponsor hip hop one-nighters. Formerly a neighborhood bar bent on hardcore, **De Duivel** has recently changed stripes and now plays only rap and hip hop tunes (okay, and occasional punk lite). Often overshadowed on Club Street, a k a Reguliersdwarsstraat, by big-name clubs a block away like Havana, Naar Boven, and Richter, this small, smoky, lively club draws a young crowd of regulars who sport backward baseball hats and bagged-out jeans and need a nightly fix. Get it while it's hot; caprice may again strike and hip hop will be gone.

Where to hear local bands... At **PH 31**, the visual and aural contrast is surreal. A stark, white room that looks like a cinematic version of heaven is the club space for hardcore punk bands spewing lyrics about killing the rich and doing it with dogs. (Doesn't anarchy require graffiti?) This small squat bar on the southern end of Vondelpark believes in the more-is-more theory of volume. Local punk and new wave bands audition their musical anger here in front of slackers, radicals, and assorted feckless youth on Thursday, Friday, and Saturday nights. Conversation is impossible, but what's there to say?

There must be no word for "rehearse" in Dutch. At **Twin Pigs Café**, just about anyone with an instrument and a desire to go public can take the stage on Tuesday nights when the mike is open. This place feels and looks like a college bar, to wit: omnipresent smell of stale beer, posters as decorative motif, crowds that make Gen Xers look geriatric. On weekends, the Twin Pigs is where local bands jam (which is an English synonym for rehearse), so the musical quality fluctuates wildly. But hey, experimentation is the hot sauce of life—right? Every night, there's live music, no cover, no pretense, and an international crowd. The nightly happy hour is from 10 to 11, when beers are half price and the budget-minded congregate. A step up the food chain for local band venues is **ARENA**, an adjunct to the Sleep-In youth hostel and one of the few places in town where you can dance to guitar music instead of techno-driven tunes with synthesized syncopation. Next door to the Korsakoff, but light years away in disposition, **De Kroeg** is a blues and rock club that has been known to induce claustrophobia. The concept of personal space is checked at the door; your exit perfume will be Eau de Neighbor. The only respite from the beer-and-blue-jean body slam can be had by squeezing your way to the bar at the back of the room, where you can still hear just fine the local bands who stop here when they're ready to launch European tours. In the states, **De Buurvrouw** would be called a dive bar, a come-as-you-are bar. Shock rock—with some punk for spice—pounds from the sound system. The guys huddled around the pool table gambling away their guilders live in the neighborhood. The bartender knows what you drink and slides it your way before you utter the request. And the frequent live performances by local B-team punk and rock bands border on spiritual experiences.

Best after 2am... Bowls of fruits that look as if they were removed from Carmen Miranda's hat sit on the small tabletops edged against the walls of **Mazzo**, a small, signless club on Rozengracht. Slides of kiwi and lemon slices flicker on the walls; two robo-babe bartenders whir fruit and firewater concoctions in blenders. It's Fruit 4 Ears (a fresh mix of juicy jives and banana grooves, says the entry ticket), the club's Monday theme night. The small club hosts theme nights that change weekly, but most play some form of house music. At midnight, the doors open and the crowd trickles in to writhe on the living room–sized dance floor or to congregate around the bar in the back. Gays in leather, men in turbans and dashikis, club kids in dreads and bellbottoms, the usual bluejeaned contingency dance to house and garage music and sit passively watching the crowd through the haze of atmospheric dry ice clouds spat intermittently from two machines. The doors of **Seymour Likely 2** don't open until midnight, and arriving before 1am is a serious groovester gaffe. Across the street from the Seymour Likely Lounge, one of A'dam's bars that has outlasted its Warholian 15 minutes, the club is friendly and relaxed, hosting a mixed-age, arty crowd where anti-fashion (slouchwear, Doc Martens, nerd plaid) rules. Inside, the entryway Betty Ford Juice Bar sells unleaded drinks and fur-lined hallways lead downstairs to bathrooms. Upstairs in a square room, a bar stripes one end, the midsized dance floor has dibs on the center space, and an alcove with couches, chairs, and tables faces the bar. Chain-link and neon are the decorative tools. Friday nights' guest DJs play highly danceable trip-hop; by 2am the dance floor is impassable and the body heat forces a sort of strip poker. The neo-classical building in the Red Light District that houses the weekend-only club **Red** looks a bit like a government building—a post office in New England or a small burg's town hall. One of Amsterdam's newest wee-hours clubs, this bilevel place plays trance and techno tunes, the kind of soundtrack that mesmerizes and stymies. No one shows up here until 3am, long after nocturnal damage has begun to take hold. The dance floor, encircled by columns, entices only a handful of people; most are herbally introspective and prefer to sit and smoke and stare into blackened space. **Naar Boven**, a calculatedly sophisticated club on Reguliersdwarsstraat, sports an urban-industrial slick interior, a bit *Blade Runner*–ish. Checkered floors, metal railings and accents, thick clouds of dry ice, copious neon irradiating the faces of the chic patrons. A dress-to-impress code is upheld here; jeans won't cut it and the women who parade though here have a whiff of *The Stepford Wives* about them. Pile on the hair products, the 24-carat accessories, the churlish expression. Dance distractedly to funk, deep house, rock, trip hop. Sip your cocktail, ponder the future of your cuticles.

Where to skate... Thursday-night subterranean skate parties at the squat **Nieuwe Silo** sound a bit like trains in the distance. The steady thrum of spinning wheels, advancing and retreating, competes with hypnotic trance music amped up to escapist levels. Ghostlike silhouettes of skaters float across the walls. If you don't come wheeled, you're out of luck; nonskaters cluster for safety on the periphery, transfixed by the inliners moving in ambient synchronicity. At **Vrieshuis Amerika**, a waterfront squat just east of Centraal Station, the skate party is also on Thursday night and skates are free for the evening, if you're willing to fork over your passport for collateral. Here the floor is shared with skateboarders in jams and high-tops, weaving through plastic cones or popping arabesques off the dozen or so ramps.

Salsa... Two Amsterdam clubs offer salsa regularly; and Latin music shows up as the sound track for an occasional theme night for some of the larger clubs (RoXy, iT, Paradiso, Melkweg). On weekends, a live salsa band sandwiches into **Canaçao Rio**, and the tiny bar just off Leidsestraat fills with South American tourists and locals who fancy Latin rhythms. On other nights, Brazilian bands, Andean pipe-playing quintets, or Mexican guitar trios in cheesy outfits take the stage. The **Latin Club** is another of the city's salsa-only clubs. Thirtysomething and fortysomething patrons nibble on tapas and crowd the dance floor in pairs, synchronized in hip-swaying rhythm. Other clubs have begun to sponsor salsa nights, including **De Kroeg**, a small and raffish rock bar with salsa on Sunday nights; **Café Meander**, a reliably funky basement hall with a seven-piece salsa band on Sunday nights; and **Rum Runners**, a tropical, Jimmy Buffett-y restaurant and bar next to Westerkerk. On Sunday nights, the margaritas flow, the faux palm trees sway, the parrots squawk, and Latin American bands play salsa tunes for a crowd heavy on the surfer dude wannabes.

Funk, blues, and soul... It's bring in da funk, bring in da noise at **Café Meander**—sort of. Live funk and blues rule most evenings at this basement-level pocket of a club just off Spui, though its Sundays are ceded to salsa (and usually dismally bereft of an audience). Between band sets, James Brown and his bad singing self rasps from the tape deck. A black and white funkaholic crowd dominated by baby boomers reaches it zenith at about 2am. But alas, they huddle in the dark bar, avoiding the miniscule dance floor as if it were viral. This is toe-tapping, shoulder-swaying territory, the kind of place you want to stop in to before you head out dancing because you're just not loose enough yet to work your moves. **Maloe Melo** bills itself as the city's "home of the blues," but the club is more a Disney version of a blues den than a gritty roadhouse where you come to listen to lusty songs of love gone bad. Its sterile interior is nonetheless intimate enough to fill you with third-hand smoke or let you count fillings in the performers' teeth. Live music every night and no cover charge insure healthy crowds, which tend to run to the touristy boomers set. It's a crap shoot with the music: though the odds favor a B-plus or an A, some nights listening to the amateur crooning can induce the blues. At **Soul Kitchen** the dress code is brief, sort of a list of *Glamour* don'ts: no shorts, no running shoes. On the yes dress list are fringe vests, Nik Nik shirts, Elton John-esque platform shoes, and any other sartorial reference to the sixties and seventies. The soundtrack dips into those two decades as well, with funk, soul, and disco piped through mondo speakers tucked into the corners of the spacious club. Grass don't grow here, friend; this is a club where people come to dance—solo, in couples, into the hours that abut daybreak. Though the sign outside **Richter** announces that the club is for members only, it's just the management's way of fashion-policing. You don't have to sport Armani or Mizrahi here, but chuck the fanny pack, the sweatpants, the UCLA T-shirt, and the Nike Airs—telltale signs of tourists—and you'll gain admittance. After you pass through a metal detector and perchance get frisked by sullen bouncers. Inside, the decor, with shards of mirror spiraling on the walls, is meant to resemble an earthquake, but the feel is Bee Gees. Two levels mean primo vantage points for surveying the preening crowds. Three bars and numerous nooks afford spots for trysting or conversation. The soundtrack vacillates between disco and soul (especially on the weekends), spun for a well-heeled, cocktail-swilling crowd who remember Sly and the Family Stone, James Brown, Etta James, and Don Cornelius.

Student dance clubs... Lolitas pout their dewy lips and shake their pubescent booties at **Dansen bij Jansen**, a student discotheque in the area between Damrak and Spui. Reportedly, no one older than 25 is allowed entry; a student card must be shown for admission, but if your alpha-hydroxy concoctions are fulfilling their pledges of younger-looking skin, maybe you can chat up the bouncer and he won't suspect a thing. The soundtrack leans toward Top 40, and the patter centers on exams, fossilized professors, and term breaks. **Amnesia** is housed on the bottom floor of a student youth hostel on the northern edge of the Red Light District. The crowds are barely post-pubescent here. Top city DJs like Dimitri, C-4, and Guido spin hardcore techno music while the young and restless gyrate with bottled beers in hand. If you must get thee to a nunnery, **ARENA** is housed in a former convent close to Oosterpark. The refurbed 400-capacity hall is an adjunct to a youth hostel, and the club tenaciously clings to its underground, unpolished, neo-Beat reputation. Obscure edge bands such as Riciotti Ensemble, Alkbottle, and Devil's Jam perform to a mostly international, just-passing-through crowd of twentysomethings sporting tattoos and nose rings, Guatemalan string bracelets and ankh necklaces—backpackers' amulets. The same crowd populates **Odeon** a multilevel bar in a 17th-century canalhouse decorated with ceiling paintings. In an upstairs concert hall, 1960s *Big Chill* music plays. On the ground floor, house tunes rule (and the crowd is thickest), and in the cellar, moodier jazz and acid jazz prevail for those who want to get stoned, forego interaction, and regard music as transportation. The club at **Winston Hotel** is also attached to a youth hostel in the Red Light District, which means it is a haunt of twentysomething backpackers who favor Euro-house tunes and dancing as "the vertical expression of horizontal desire," as Oscar Wilde put it. In addition to music, the entertainment is akin to the mixed bag of "The Gong Show", with poetry readings on Monday nights, rock-and-roll comedy theater on weekend nights, theme parties, and live band performances.

In the Red Lights... Titillation in many variations is big commerce in Amsterdam. You don't need a guidebook to ferret out a shamelessly over-the-top sex show: subtlety is anathema to this sort of show biz. Beefy hawkers stand before sleazy clubs in the District, drumming up business. Oversized photos of bare-breasted women in various come-hither poses adorn the storefronts. Colored lights throb. Triple X's reveal all. The city's most notorious and popular (you'll most likely be seated next to a grandmotherly type, maybe a family) is **Casa Rosso**, a theater featuring explicit action on stage: ridiculous props, lingerie, couples, threesomes, audience participation. Think X-rated Disney World (even though it's not a small world, after all). In the same neighborhood, and operated by the same porno purveyors, is a sex club for those with a thing for one of the food groups called **Bananenbar.** Red Light District. Naked women on stage. Bananas. You do the math, Cheetah.

A walk on the wild(er) side... Continuing on the theme of tolerance, the public practice of sado-masochism is legal here. Given the range of possibilities, the city's two publicly listed and advertised S/M clubs, **Hellen's Place** (skewed toward lesbian S/M) and **G-Force** (theme nights, fetish parties, standard-issue S/M clientele), are S/M lite: moderate pain, humiliation, and cruelty. The general scene includes spanking, whipping, playing the role of dominatrix or dominator, wearing a hood, mewling, cowering, performing sex acts on the demand of the master. Locals say there is a more hard-core S/M scene, but it remains underground and unadvertised. Inquire at the two clubs for more information; G-Force also publishes a monthly listing of S/M and fetish happenings around town.

Down an alley off Warmoesstraat in the Red Light District, **G-Force** calls itself an S/M-friendly cafe, though it seems part recreational and part educational. Patrons are more than willing to discuss the nuances of pain-for-pleasure. While a dominatrix whips a dog-collared slave, she shouts commands and intructs passers-by about the finer points of domination. S/M magazines sit on the bar and on clusters of tables where people converse and survey. Soft-core S/M videos blink on corner monitors, and artwork à la Robert Mapplethorpe and Helmut Newton adorns the walls. A trapdoor behind the bar leads to a dungeon with a display that looks as if it was borrowed from the torture museum. The bar sponsors theme parties with evenings for couples, women only, fetish fanciers (every Thursday), or those under 25. If you don't wear something leather, mildly militaristic, or sport body piercing on your torso, you'll likely feel out of place. The curious are welcome, but anyone bent on proselytizing and judging will be escorted out. **Hellen's Place**, a "woman-friendly erotic cafe," is run by a woman and has a dark room, a specific kind of dark room for anonymous encounters, of the erotic kind, mixed with gays and straights. Saturday nights are when the place reaches its apex, with a bouillabaisse of transvestites, lesbians, straights, fetishists, exhibitionists, and gays. A man wearing a dog collar and a noose around his neck circulates through the crowd, while a quartet of butch dykes in leather hats and thigh-high boots take turns biting each other. Not for the squeamish or prudish.

For folkies... Amsterdam's folk scene doesn't thrive the way its rock and jazz counterparts do, and the few places that feature folk are generally more sedate and frequented by people over 30. **Mulligan's** on the Amstel is the quintessential Irish pub, with Guinness on tap, a laconic bartender prone to quoting Yeats to the lovelorn, a homey feel, and the requisite live folk music—much of it Gaelic and Celtic—on Friday and Saturday nights. The interior looks like a wood-paneled den. You know it's adios time when

THE CLUB SCENE ⟨ THE LOWDOWN

someone requests "When Irish Eyes Are Smiling." In the same vein, **The Blarney Stone**, just west of Centraal Station, pulls the same sort of crowd to the same sort of authentically worn-in Irish bar where the same musicians play cry-in-your-beer tunes to lit expats. In the midst of the city's Off-Off-Broadway theater street, Nes, **De String** is a wee bit of a club that features folk unplugged every evening. Because the performance space is so miniscule, this is a folk venue for solo performers—a harpist, an acoustic guitarist, a flutist, maybe with an accompanying crooner—and the music serves much like Muzak piping in the background. During the day, some of the performers take their tunes to the street and play in Leidseplein or in front of Centraal Station for the random guilders passersby drop into their cups. De String patrons tend to be earnest theatergoers who favor lively post-curtain conversation and controlling their alcoholic beverage intake.

Squat clubs... The squat club/restaurant/dance hall/apartment/performance space scene is unique to Amsterdam. City law says that if a building remains empty for more than a year without the owner somehow utilizing it, the space can be squatted, that is, people can move in and use it until the building sells. The law was created to protect the city from speculators who may be inclined to exploit the city's keen housing shortage by sitting on their property and watching the price rise. While the condition of these reclaimed buildings can be one step up from condemnable, some squat bars and cafes are indistinguishable from those with the traditional landlord/tenant relationship. Some see patronizing squats as a show of solidarity, a political gesture that somehow shoots the finger at The Man and confirms an ethos generated in the sixties subculture of the U.S. **Vrankrijk**, on Spuistraat, has molted from an anarchist's squat bar where weekend parties featured head-banging punk bands, lethal mosh pits, and pallid youth in combat boots and perma-sneers. Today, it's got a whiff of its angry genesis—a sign above the door reads, "No Nazis, No Yuppies, No Cameras," the exterior of the building is splashed with trippy inner-city graffiti, and the music still runs toward heavy metal and punk—but the atmosphere has taken a Prozac. Mellow groups of twentysomethings and their dogs sit at tables. The proletariat Talking Heads sneak onto the soundtrack. Nights pass without a fistfight. A group of obvious tourists stumbles in and no one blinks when one of them bums a cigarette and starts talking a bit too loudly in New Yawk accents. The times, they are a-changing. **Itonia** is a gonzo, neo-Beat performance space-*cum*-club where the focal point is guerilla-street filmmaking. Open only on Wednesdays, this small squat club hosts an open stage with a theme that changes weekly. Onstage: poetry readings, improvisational dance, plays, bands—mostly in English (as the squat is run by two renegade Aussies.) When the night begins, audience members head outside with minicams and return to show their film before evening's end. In a dingy basement of another squat building, **De Trut** hosts a Sunday night gay disco. The decor is low-budget squat, with exposed rafters, peeling paint, bare light bulbs, pockmarked floors. The sound system is stellar, the decibels high, and the dance floor packed enough that the club shuts its door at about midnight when the occupancy reaches saturation.

The hippest squat club in town at the moment is **Nieuwe Silo**, out by the docks west of Centraal Station. A squat collective pioneered by a group of artists, the building houses living and working spaces upstairs; downstairs is a late, late-night club with weekend Radical Groover raves that don't get going until 3 or 4am. A favorite among bartenders, waitrons, and assorted anarchist ravers, the basement club includes a bar, a smartdrink counter, clusters of couches, and an oversized circular furnace. On Thursday nights, the place becomes a skating rink where in-liners weave and twirl to trance tunes, dodging the pylons and the clots of dancers. The Silo also hosts "Inrichting Alternative Dance Night," a bimonthly goth gathering where the night creatures gather to vamp and prowl, powdered white and attired in black. Just east of Centraal Station is **Vrieshuis Amerika**, a six-story waterfront walk-up on Het IJ advertised only via fliers and word of mouth. The elaborate space mimics an oversized, otherworldly fun house. Friday raves begin at midnight on the top floor; the crowd is heavily international-backpacker. The third floor of the building is a skatepark with elaborate ramps and the everpresent whir of wheels on wood, as hardcore in-liners and skateboarders master their moves. Bottom floors have been squatted by artists who live and work in the building; there's even crash space on the second floor for broke travelers seeking shelter for a night. The **Onafhankelijk Cultureel Centrum** is a 12-year-old mainstream squat space that is a one-stop shop for culture vultures. Inside are a sauna, cabaret, bar, dance floor, stage, art gallery, and Kasbah cafe. House, rap, and trance music waft across a dance floor that holds a couple hundred writhers. In the downstairs cabaret, some earnest soul reads poetry while his sidekick plays Andean pipes. Neon-colored sculptures of tree roots sit on pedestals dotted about the building. With faces flushed from a detoxing sauna, some stumble upstairs to the Kasbah to quaff Spa Red mineral water and regain their electrolyte balance.

Gambling... The city's only official casino is **Holland Amsterdam Casino**, just a roll of the dice away from Leideseplein (geographically, not spiritually). The standard games—roulette, blackjack, craps—are played in the standard casino decor: clockless, overlit, neon in hyperdrive, bells, and whistles. The slots are always busy with forlorn characters, coin-filled paper cups at hand, yanking the metallic limb of the one-armed bandit with resolution and a prayer.

World music... Amsterdam's world music scene has been influenced by the influx of sizeable immigrant populations from Indonesia, Suriname, West Africa, and Turkey, all of whom have weaved their musical traditions, instruments, and syncopation into European rock. It's little wonder world music, the sound of the global village, has caught fire in the international city of Amsterdam. The acknowledged world music center here is **Akhnaton**, a multicultural youth center that encourages and supports world music, particularly from Africa, the Caribbean, and Arabic-speaking nations. Akhnaton is a down-home hangout popular with the city's established international populations. The venue includes a recording studio, rehearsal spaces for roots-rock bands, and a club that—Fridays and Saturdays only—hosts hip hop performances, salsa parties, world music fests, rap festivals, ska and soca fiestas, African raves (Les Nuites Africaines), and more. A Rainbow Coalition crowd shakes its braids on the dance floor, and the live salsa parties, some would say, are the harbinger of another Sodom and Gomorra. A more formal venue for world music is **Soetrijn**, a theater next door to the **Tropeninsituut** (see The Arts Scene). The usual fare here is world music concerts performed by bands from developing countries. **De Bochel** is an off-the-beaten-path club, barely bigger than a dorm room, that hosts African dance parties weekend nights. An occasional post-concert dance or club night is added to the bill. **Paradiso**, the club hewn from a 17th-century church, hosts world music nights as part of their theme-night approach and **Melkweg**, the center for alternative arts, hosts June's annual World Roots Festival, featuring African and Caribbean bands.

Where the boys are... The gay club and bar scene centers on four gay ghettos: Reguliersdwarsstraat, Warmoesstraat, Kerkstraat, and Amstel. Holding court on Amstelstraat is, without debate, the best-known Amsterdam gay club, where debauchery is quotidian and exhibitionist gay culture rules: **iT**. Gender-bender celebs like Grace Jones, Jean-Paul Gaultier, and David Bowie are routine drop-ins, and the city's splendiferous transvestites parade through regularly in boas, sequins, and enough Maybelline to make over Euro Disney. The club holds 1,100 people and fills with a trend-o-matic, peacocking gay and straight crowd Thursday, Friday, and Sunday nights: leather, dog collars, Spandex, pierced nipples, platforms—in short, contagious outrageous. Dancers in cages are suspended from the ceiling; pumping house and high energy garage tunes dominate the sound track. Saturday night is boyz only and the ultimate homo hangout. Reguliersdwarsstraat has two extremely popular gay clubs—**April's Exit**, or "Exit" as locals call it, and **Havana**. Both are cruisy and heavily gay but draw mixed crowds on weekends. **Havana** is usually the first stop for clubhoppers because the place gets juiced at about midnight, doesn't have a cover charge, and shuts down at 2am. Art deco, Hollywood style, prevails in the club's pastels, its plants, and the curve and pad of its furniture. Conversation is the lubricant here and chattering, cruising hordes spill onto the street, eschewing the small upper-level dance floor. Down the street, **Exit** doesn't lift off until about 1am. The three main stories hold humungous dance floors. Curaçao-blue light radiates from an upstairs bar, and in the basement is the darkroom, where a sign forbids women to enter, cautions against pickpockets, and suggests safe sex only. Locals wryly call Warmoesstraat "Rue de Vaseline." The street snakes through the Red Light District and is home to the raunchier gay clubs, heavy on leather and butch vibes.

Cockring, one of Amsterdam's longest-running leather clubs, is *always* solely a male domain, and manly men only, please. Muscle-buffed men in motorcycle wear, spiked collars, boots, dead-cow trousers, and vests strut through the darkened rooms, intently cruising. On Sunday, the gay hot spot is **De Trut**, a makeshift club in the basement of a squat building. Instead of a cruise zone, this place engenders more of a party atmosphere where people dance as if they're releasing inner demons and their accumulations of urban stress. It's Gucci gays who are awarded admittance to **Homolulu**, a small Kerkstraat restaurant and nightclub. The interior is a throwback to the clubs of the forties and fifties with linen tablecloths, padded chairs, and a refined atmosphere. Owned by lesbians, the club attracts both gays and straights and sponsors monthly women-only parties.

Where the girls are... Amsterdam has no women-only dance clubs and only one women-only bar—**Cafe Saarein** (see The Bar and Cafe Scene) in Jordaan. Instead, the city's lesbian party population is a nomadic lot, making pilgrimages to clubs that sponsor weekly or monthly lesbian-friendly parties, raves, and gatherings. Places for party information include the bulletin board at Cafe Saarein; **Xantippe** (Prinsengracht 290, tel 020/623–5854), the largest women's bookstore in Europe; the bulletin board at **Het Vrouwenhuis** (Nieuwe Herengracht 95, tel 020/625–2066), headquarters of two feminist magazines and the Dutch Women's Movement; and listings inside gay/lesbian publications such as *Trash in the Streets*, free and distributed in clubs; *GayKrant*, a weekly gay newspaper with listings; and *Gay Times*, a British monthly with club updates. The COC is a progressive government-sponsored gay rights organization. The Amsterdam branch is a social nexus for gay and lesbian activities and a pulse point for info about gay and lesbian parties. It sponsors the Saturday night **COC Disco**, a lesbian-only mixer. A wide stripe of women congregate here, mixed in age, politics, and fashion. The mission seems more about networking than cruising—until the wee hours, when decibels rise, crowds reach critical mass, shirts come off, and the dance floor mutates into a lovefest. The Sunday night *Pussy Lounge* upstairs at **RoXy**, the city's über-cool club, attracts mostly lipstick lesbians coiffed and cosmeticized into *Vogue* versions of beauty. The crowd is peppered with what some locals call "viral lesbians" (they'll do women for about 48 hours), and the scene is cruise and pose. In Amsterdam, the roving Clit Club can be found at the **Web Club**, where every Friday night the girls who like girls outnumber the boys who like boys.

Comedy clubs... The aptly named **Comedy Club** (if they're so funny, why can't they come up with a more clever name?) hosts comedy gigs nightly with four shows on Fridays and Saturdays. Most of the performing yuk-meisters at this small club aim for silliness in Dutch and lampoon Dutch politicians, so without fluidity in the language all but the few sight gags will sail over your head. Usually, only an occasional English-speaking comedian will drop in from England, the U.S., Australia, or New Zealand, drawing laugh-deprived countrymen. During the summers, however, comedy shows in English are a regular weekly feature, with much of the humor leaning toward slapstick or, à la Seinfeld, a what's-up-with-that befuddlement with mundane human behavior.

The Index

Alto Jazz Café. Smoky nook off the neon jungle of the Leidseplein. Live nightly jazz draws a friendly, mixed-age crowd of locals and tourists.... *Tel 020/626–3249. Korte Leidsedwarsstraat 115; tram 1, 2, 5, 6, 7, 10, or 11. Open until 4am.*

Akhnaton. World music with a playlist that favors Latin and African and a dance floor that looks like a Benetton ad. Crowd heavy on dreads, body piercings, and the glassy eyes of hash intake.... *Tel 020/624–3396. Nieuwezijds Kolk 25; tram 1, 2, 5, 11, 13, or 17. Open until 1am. Closed Sun–Thur.*

Amnesia. Small, student-oriented club on ground floor of Red Light District youth hostel.... *Tel 020/638–1461. Oudezijds Voorburgwal 3; tram 4, 9, 14, 16, 24, or 25. Open until 4am Thur and Sun, until 5am Fri and Sat. Closed Mon–Wed. Cover charge.*

April's Exit. Slick, high-tech, three-story gay disco with a no-women-allowed sex area called the darkroom.... *Tel 020/625–8788. Reguliersdwarsstraat 42; tram 1, 2, 5, or 11. Open daily until 5am. Cover charge.*

ARENA. Youth hostel club thronged with undulating twenty-somethings, mostly backpackers.... *Tel 020/694–744. 's Gravesandestraat 51; tram 6, 7, or 10. Open until 3am. Closed Mon–Wed. Cover charge.*

Bamboo Bar. A "Gilligan's Island" tiki motif and a twenty- and thirtysomething crowd pack this small bar where there's live music nightly and a saltine-sized dance floor.... *Tel 020/624–3993. Lange Leidsedwarsstraat 115; tram 1, 2, 5, 6, 7, 10, or 11. Open until 3am. Closed Sun.*

Bananenbar. Erotic, seedy, tourist-trappy Red Light District club where monkeys' favorite fruit becomes public erotic device for nude, undulating women.... *Tel 020/627–8945 or 020/622–4670. Oudezijds Achterburgwal 106 and 37; tram 4, 9, 16, 24, or 25. Open until 3am. Cover charge.*

Bimhuis. The city's landmark jazz club for the last two decades. Cavernous interior, older crowds, and top-name jazz acts.... *Tel 020/623–1361. Oude Scans 73; tram 9 or 14, Metro Nieuwmarkt. Open until 3am. Cover charge.*

The Blarney Stone. A small, mossy Irish pub with live Celtic music...*Tel 020/623–3830. Nieuwendijk 29; tram 4, 9, 16, 24, or 25. Open until 2am. Closed Mon–Wed.*

De Bochel. Small, dark club on the edge of city center with world music dance parties on weekends.... *Tel 020/693–2025. Andreas Bonnstraat 28, Metro Weesperplein. Open until 5am. Cover charge.*

Bourbon Street. More Marvin Hamlisch than Miles Davis from the nightly live jazz and Dixieland bands.... *Tel 020/623–3440. Leidsekruisstraat 6; tram 1, 2, 5, 6, 7, 10, or 11. Open until 4am.*

De Buurvrouw. Miniscule bar/club with a pool table, local rock band performances, and a prediliction for alternative and punk music.... *Tel 020/625–9654. Pieterpoortsteeg 9; tram 4, 9, 14, 16, 24, or 25. Open until 2am Mon–Thur, until 3am Fri–Sat. Closed Sun.*

Café Meander. Funk, jazz, acid jazz, and blues on small side street that draws a thirtysomething crowd to the smoky, dimly lit, basement-level club. Salsa bands Sundays.... *Tel 020/625–8430. Voetboogstraat 3; tram 1, 2, 5, 11, 13, or 17. Open until 3am.*

Casa Rosso. Cheesy sex club in the Red Light District with live sex acts on stage and audience participation encouraged.... *Tel 020/627–8945. Oudezijds Achterburgwal 106; trams 4, 9, 16, 24, or 25. Open until 3am. Cover charge.*

Caneçao Rio. Brazilian music bar with live salsa on weekends and a hip-swaying crowd of locals and South American turistas…. *Tel 020/626–1500. Lange Leidsedwarstraat 68; tram 1, 2, 5, or 11. Open until 5am.*

Cash. Glitzy Leidseplein disco. A whiff of Atlantic City neon and lamé and inside a crowd right out of *Saturday Night Fever…. Tel 020/627–6544. Leidseplein 12; tram 1, 2, 5, 6, 7, 10, or 11. Open until 4am. Cover charge.*

Catacomb Studio. Home of Fetish Faction, the last Saturday of the month. An erotically charged fetish party for initiates only. Dress right or don't come!… *Tel 020/697–8094. Haarlemmerstraat 124C, bus 18 or 22. Open until 5am.*

COC Disco. Rowdy weekend party sponsored by COC, the government-subsidized gay rights organization…*Tel 020/623–4079. Rozenstraat 14; tram 13, 14, or 17. Open Fri until 4am (mixed gay and lesbian), Sat until 3am (lesbian only). Closed Sun–Thur. Cover charge.*

Cockring. Crowded, sweaty, way gay club that is one of the city's longest-running leather clubs…. *Tel 020/623–9604. Warmoesstraat 96; tram 4, 9, 16, 24, or 25. Open until 4am Mon–Thur, until 5am Fri–Sun. Men only; cover charge.*

Comedy Club. International comedy acts perform, and a summer series sponors English-speaking yukmeisters…. *Tel 020/638–3971. Max Euweplein 29; tram 1, 2, 5, or 11. Shows 11pm Tue–Sun, 9 and 11:30pm Sat. Closed Mon. Cover charge.*

Dansen bij Jansen. College-student, shake-your-booty dance house where no one over 25 is admitted…. *Tel 020/620–1779. Handboogstraat 11; tram 1, 2, 5, or 11. Open until 5am. Entry only with student card; cover charge.*

De Duivel. Rap and hip-hop music (one of the few places in town to hear both regularly). Weekend nights this is gangsta turf minus the menace…. *Tel 020/626–6184. Reguliersdwarsstraat 87; tram 1, 2, 5, or 11. Open until 2am Sun–Thur, until 3am Fri–Sat.*

Escape. A-list, dress-to-impress disco with lines that snake for blocks on Friday and Saturday nights around 2am…. *Tel 020/62–3542. Rembrandtplein 11; tram 4, 9, or 14. Open until 4am Thur, until 5am Fri–Sat. Closed Sun–Wed. Cover charge.*

G-Force. S/M sex club in the Red Light District for the pleasure/ pain curious and the committed. Ouch.... *Tel 020/420– 1664. Oudezijds Armsteeg 7; tram 1, 2, 4, 5, 9, 11, 13, 17, 24, or 25. Open until midnight.*

Havana. Noisy, cruisy, dishy, way gay club with boyz, butch types, queens, dear queers.... *Tel 020/620–6788. Reguliersdwarsstraat 17; tram 1, 2, 5, 16, 24, or 25. Open until 1am Sun–Mon and Thu, until 2am Fri–Sat. Closed Tue–Wed.*

Hellen's Place. Billed as a women's erotic cafe, this S/M club is a dim and discreet gathering place for just about everyone on the sexual fringes: swingers, gays, lesbians, bis, transvestites.... *Tel 020/689–5501. Overtoom 497, tram 1 or 6. open until 1am Sun–Thur, until 2am Fri–Sat.*

Holland Amsterdam Casino. The city's only official casino frequented by tour bus crowds in sequins.... *Tel 020/620– 1006. Max Euweplein 62; tram 1, 2, 5, 6, 7, 10, or 11. Open until 3am daily.*

Homolulu. Lesbian-owned but gay-frequented nightclub and restaurant for the well-dressed, moneyed strata.... *Tel 020/ 624–6387. Kerkstraat 23; tram 1, 2, 5, or 11. Open until 4am Tue–Thur and Sun, until 5am Fri–Sat. Closed Mon.*

iT. Poser central, this unabashedly flamboyant gay disco has a mixed crowd (except on Saturdays, when it's boys only), churlish bartenders, and eye-popping people-watching. The place doesn't reach full throttle until about 4am.... *Tel 020/ 625–0111. Amstelstraat 24; tram 4, 9, or 14. Open until 5am. Closed Mon–Tue. Cover charge.*

Itonia. Tiny, arty, Wednesday-only squat club with an open stage: poetry readings, live music, extemporaneous theater, guerilla film fests—and mostly in English.... *No telephone. Kloveniersburgwal 20; tram 4, 9, or 14. Open from 10pm until caprice dictates. Closed Thur–Tue.*

Joseph Lam Jazz Club. *Louche*, smoky, funk-woven jazz club for the goateed, filterless-cigarette-smoking, beret-wearing crowd.... *Tel 020/622–8086. Van Diemenstraat 8, tram 3 to terminus then bus 35. Open weekends only. Cover charge on Sat.*

THE INDEX ⟋ THE CLUB SCENE

Korsakoff. Punk-rock place where grunge is alive and thriving. Anarchist clubwear, tattoos, and palpable ennui lace the acrid air. For the very young, the very angry…. *Tel 020/625–7854. Lijnbaansgracht 161; tram 6, 7, 10, 13, 14, or 17. Open until 1am Sun–Thur, until 2am Fri–Sat. Occasional cover charge.*

De Kroeg. Blues and rock place, smells like European armpits…. *Tel 020/420–0232. Lijnbaansgracht 163; tram 7, 10, 13, 14, or 17. Open until 3am. Closed Mon–Tue. Cover charge.*

Latin Club. Small grown-ups' cocktail bar with live salsa bands and tapas…. *Tel 020/624–2270. Oudezijds Voorburgwal 254; tram 4, 9, 16, 24, or 25. Open until 2am Sun–Thur, until 3am Fri–Sat.*

Lido. The disco in the Holland Casino with a kitschy Holiday Inn–lounge atmosphere that the patrons mistake for glamour…. *Tel 020/620–1006. Max Euweplein 62; tram 1, 2, 5, 6, 7, or 11. Open until 3am. Cover charge.*

Maloe Melo. Blues cafe with nightly live music. A fortysomething crowd clusters around the tables and applauds ferociously…. *Tel 020/420–4592. Lijnbaansgracht 163; tram 6, 7, 10, 13, 14, or 17. Open until 2am.*

Marcanti Plaza. Host to Amsterdam's version of the Bridge & Tunnel crowd (big hair, cheap shoes, intermittent lapses in grammar), Saturdays only…. *Tel 020/682–3456. Jan van Galenstraat 6–8, tram 3. Open until 5am. Closed Sun–Fri. Cover charge.*

Mazzo. House tunes, theme nights, clubkid central, fashion laissez-faire…. *Tel 020/626–7500. Rozengracht 114; tram 13, 14, or 17. Open from 11:30pm until 5am. Cover charge.*

Melkweg. Former dairy converted into megaspace that has been at forefront of Amsterdam nightlife scene for more than 20 years. A venue for big-time visiting acts and a packed club favored by backpackers and Gen Xers…. *Tel 020/624–8492. Lijnbaansgracht 234; tram 1, 2, 5, 6, 7, 10, or 11. Open until 5am. Cover charge.*

Mulligan's. Live Celtic music Wednesday through Saturday nights in the most cheery of the Irish bars in town. Favored by expats. Guinness on tap.... *Tel 020/622–1330. Amstel 100; tram 4, 9, or 14. Open until 2am.*

Naar Boven. Recorded funk, hardcore rock, and trip-hop music in this stylish, sleek club frequented by fashion plates.... *Tel 020/623–3981. Reguliersdwarsstraat 12; tram 1, 2, 5, or 11. Open until 4am Sun–Thur, until 5am Fri–Sat.*

Nieuwe Silo. Late-night dance club on west side near the docks. Raves on weekends, Thursday nights for skaters, goth parties second Saturday of the month... *Tel 020/625–0561. Westerdoksdijk 51, bus 35. Open Thur–Sat 11pm–5am. Cover charge.*

Odeon. Three floors with balconies that perch over a dance floor sardined with a crowd that just started shaving.... *Tel 020/624–9711. Singel 460; tram 1, 2, 5, or 11. Open until 4am Sun–Thur, until 5am Fri–Sat. Cover charge.*

Onafhankelijk Cultureel Centrum. Arty, squat space with dance hall, bar, stage, sauna, and cafe... *Tel 020/671–7778. Amstelveenseweg 134, tram 6. Open until 2am. Closed (sometimes) in August.*

Paradiso. The doyenne of the club scene for concerts and dancing. Where visiting rockers come to perform.... *Tel 020/623–7348. Weteringschans 6–8; tram 1, 2, 5, 6, 7, 10, or 11. Hours and cover charge vary nightly with program.*

PH 31. Squat club with live music Wed and Thur nights.... *Tel 020/673–6850. Prins Hendriklaan 31, tram 2. Open until 3am. Closed Sun–Tue.*

Red. Zonked-out, weekend-only dance club playing trance and techno house music.... *Tel 020/420–0626. Oude Zijds Voorburgwal 216; tram 4, 9, 16, 24, or 25. Open until 5am. Cover charge.*

Richter. Top 40, disco, soul, and occasional trance music at this club that's jammed nightly. Live music on occasional weekends.... *Tel 020/626–1573. Reguliersdwarsstraat 36; tram*

1, 2, 5, or 11. Open until 4am Mon–Thur, until 5am Fri–Sat. Closed Sun. Cover charge.

RoXy. One of the few clubs with a dress code (no sneakers, torn jeans, T-shirts, slouchwear), with a membership fee, and with attitude potential from the doorman. Packed and popular with jet-setters, local lovelies, rock-star wanna-bes. Wednesday is gay night.... *Tel 020/620–0354. Singel 465; tram 1, 2, 4, 5, 9, 11, 16, or 24. Open until 4am Wed–Thur and Sun, until 5am Fri–Sat. Closed Mon–Tue. Cover charge.*

Rum Runners. Lethal cocktails sate the Hawaiian-shirt crowd heavy on the frat-boy *joie de vivre*. Live salsa bands on Sunday nights.... *Tel 020/627–4079. Prinsengracht 277, tram 13 or 17. Open until midnight Mon–Thur, until 2am Fri–Sat. Closed Sun.*

Seymour Likely 2. Ultra-groovy post-midnight bar o' the moment. Filled with hipsters of all ages dancing experimen-tally.... *Tel 020/420–5062. Nieuwzijds Voorburgwal 161; tram 1, 2, 5, 11, or 17. Open midnight–4am Thur and Sun, until 5am Fri–Sat. Closed Mon–Wed. Cover charge.*

Soeterijn. World folk music in an intimate theater attached to the Tropenmuseum.... *Tel 020/568–8200. Linnaeusstraat 2; tram 9, 10, or 14. Hours vary depending on performance.*

Soul Kitchen. Best as an after-club club because the crowds don't rev up until about 3am. Funk and soul (thus the name) rule the soundtrack. Dance music here also dips into blues and a spot of jazz. Active dance floor that rages when James Brown kicks a tune. Peak time between 3am and closing.... *No telephone. Amstelstraat 32; tram 4, 9, or 14. Open until 5am Fri–Sat. Closed Sun–Thur. Cover charge.*

De String. Folk music, men with beards, Birkenstock territo-ry.... *Tel 020/625–9015. Nes 98; tram 4, 9, 14, 16, 24, or 25. Open until 2am Sun–Thur, until 3am Fri–Sat.*

De Trut. Dingy basement squat club goes gay disco on Sunday nights. Mardi Gras atmosphere, Trekkie-inspired clubwear, unfettered revelry.... *Tel 020/612–3524. Bilderkijkstraat 165; tram 3, 7, 12, or 17. Open until 5am.*

Twin Pigs Café. International crowd gathers to hear live music performed by local bands. Tuesday is open mike night and happy hour is 10 to 11pm.... *Tel 020/624–9516. Nieuwendijk 100; tram 1, 2, 5, 11, 13, or 17. Open until 3am Sun–Thur, until 4am Fri–Sat.*

Vrankrijk. Casual squatter bar with graffitied exterior and small red sign. Ring buzzer for entry into poster-plastered, high-ceilinged room filled with smoke, angry young men, and their dogs....*No telephone. Spuistraat 216; tram 1, 2, 5, or 11. Open until 4am.*

Vrieshuis Amerika. Squat funhouse near Centraal Station with a skatepark, exhibition space, and Friday night raves on the top floor.... *Tel 020/668–4252. Oostelijke Hanledskade 25; bus 28, 32, or 39. Open until whenever.*

Wb Club. Current home of the roving Clit Club, the women-only party held on Friday nights.... *Tel 020/624–8764. Oude Zijdsvoorburgwal 15–17; tram 4, 9, 16, 24, or 25. Open until 5am. Closed Sat–Thur. Women only.*

Winston Hotel. Recently renovated student hotel in Red Light District hosts nightly parties—poetry, comedy, improv theater. Afterwards, chairs are pushed aside for some heavy-duty dancing.... *Tel 020/623–1380. Warmoesstraat 123–129; all trams and buses to Centraal Station, Metro Centraal Station. Open until 3am. Cover charge.*

the bar and

cafe scene

It doesn't take a rocket scientist to deduce that beer is the libation of choice in the city that spawned Heineken and Amstel. Since the Middle Ages, Amsterdammers have chosen the wheat drink in lieu of the local drinking water, which was often contaminated. Today the water's fine, but you're still more likely to hear a local ordering *een pils* (a beer) rather than a cocktail in cafes, bars, and restaurants. It's not as simple and straightforward as it sounds, though: what you need to know from the outset is that not every Dutch beer is created equal. Local lagers are called *pils*, the omnipresent brands being Grolsch, Heineken, Amstel, and Oranjeboom. A strong gold color, *pils* is served in a slender slip of a glass with a head of foam two fingers wide. Some lagers are cued to the seasons: Popular in summer is *witbier*, a lighter colored brew tinged with a citrusy aftertaste and often served with a lemon slice. *Bokbier*, which appears each fall, is about midway between *witbier* and dark beer in color and alcohol content. (It's actually the Belgians who brew the heartiest dark beers, but say this *sotto voce* around the Dutch; order a De Konnick or a potent Duvel if you want to get whirly downing just one.)

Cafes

Amsterdammers drink beer in various kinds of cafes as well as in bars; in this city you'll find that the word cafe applies to a wide range of establishments. A so-called "brown cafe," or *bruine kroeg*, is a cozier and less seedy version of an American neighborhood bar. The designation "brown" (as opposed to neo-brown, grand, designer, or white) refers to the predominant color scheme, achieved in most of these places via the patina of the wood furniture, bar top, and walls, and from years of tobacco smoke. Other distinguishing features: delicate curlicue type on the outside windows, casual dress code, bar food, uncreepy, neighborhood folk, no poseurs, and minimal decor. If late-night drinking is what you're after, brown cafes fit the bill—they're open until 2 or 3am. Neo-brown means the cafe is straining for the history, authenticity, and *gezelligheid* (familiar coziness) of a brown, but has instead gone the faux route, sort of like buying a distressed new pair of blue jeans. There's no shortcutting the genuine wear of time. On the other end of the cafe spectrum are the anti-browns, known interchangeably as grand, designer, or white cafes. These modern, spacious, and purposefully decorated cafes serve the same purpose as their brown kin, but their packaging is classier, their menus more extensive, and their clientele tilted heavily toward hipsters and yuppies under 45. A potent firewater specifically associated with Amsterdam is *genever*, which some call Dutch gin. Distilled from molasses, this clear, potent liquor is available undressed or in fruit and herb flavors. Variety extends to age as well: Look for *oude*, *jonge*, or *zeer oud*—"old," "young," or "very old." As the stuff ages, the flavor mellows and the price rises. The Dutch drink *genever* neat, often with a beer chaser (called a *calaatje pils*). The reverse process—chasing a *pils* with a *genever*—is known as a *kopstoot*. Traditionally, the best place to taste *genever* was in *proeflokalen* or "tasting houses." These establishments first appeared in the mercantile landscape in the 17th century so spirits importers would have a place where merchants could sample their wares. Today *genever* isn't solely the realm of *proeflokalen;* it sits in bars and cafes alongside Scotch, tequila, and vodka. Even if you've sworn off the hard stuff, a visit to a *proeflokaal* makes for a quintessentially Dutch field trip. But hurry—tasting houses may be an endangered species; their numbers seem to be dwindling annually.

Smoking Coffeeshops

For other kinds of highs, there's also "Dutch brandy," but don't go there, friends. Trust the research. The public availability and blasé tolerance of marijuana and hashish have earned Amsterdam notoriety and praise among the herbally inclined. Slippery legal wording allows possession of small amounts of the soft drugs (but it doesn't condone purchase or sale). The apt Dutch term for this special status is *dogen*, which means "illegal but allowed." More than 450 so-called smoking coffeeshops dot the city streets. Coffee is in fact available inside, but rarely anything stronger when it comes to *liquid* refreshment; few smoking coffeeshops have liquor licenses. What really brings in the crowds is the menu of pot, hash, or "skunk" (the Dutch-grown weed known as *nederwiet*). All of these goodies are available by the gram or in pre-rolled joints. Some smoking coffeeshops also sell space cakes and electric bonbons, but these seem to be declining in popularity, maybe due in part to the healthy-living fascism that has crept over here from the States. Several telltale signs differentiate these establishments from the kind frequented by Junior Leaguers on a break from an exhausting afternoon of retail therapy: For one thing the smoking variety spell "coffeeshop" as one word; you'll see it emblazoned on storefronts and signs. There is no Dutch word for smoking coffeeshop; the words "coffee" and "shop" fused together indicate that herbs are sold inside along with java. The exterior paint jobs on these joints tend to be heavy on the primary colors; most of the names sound as if they were dreamed up by stoned surfer dudes—copious references to Bob Marley, Jamaica, or counterculture (Rasta Baby, Mellow

Yellow, Josephine Baker)—and then, of course there's the tell-tale treacly scent of burning hashish.

Neighborhoods

Amsterdam neighborhoods offer an array of bar scenes. The one on **Warmoesstraat**, just north of the Red Light District, is leather gay and cruisy. **Kerkstraat**, a couple of side streets off **Rembrandtplein**, and **Club-Central** near **Reguliersdwarsstraat**, two other gay districts, are not quite as intimidating and wide open to straights as well. **Cafe Saarein**, in the artistic enclave of **Jordaan**, is the only women-only lesbian bar, though cafes and bars in the gay ghettos are popular with lesbians as well. The touristy public squares **Leidseplein, Rembrandtplein**, and **Thorbeckeplein** are obvious, overlit, and overvisited; while these areas offer the highest concentration of nightlife in the city, their wide range of restaurants and clubs geared toward visitors—street hawkers, menus printed in four languages—means a dearth of the Dutch. Despite its salacious commerce, the Red Light District is busy and safe; its streets are in fact often paralyzed by gaggles of ogling out-of-towners, drunken Italian university boys, and camcorder-wielding Midwesterners on an AARP trip. The bars in the 'hood tend to be on the rowdy side. **De Pijp** is part of the **New South**, a funky neighborhood reminiscent of New York's Greenwich Village or Paris' Marais; its bars and cafes attract those who still remember when Paul McCartney was with the Beatles. Avant-garde theater flourishes around Nes, one of the main arteries of the **Oude Zijds** area, just east of the Red Light District. After the performances the appropriately quirky audiences descend on the area's many artsy cafes to throw back a few drinks and argue about exactly what it was they just saw. Visitors to **Jordaan** are soon smitten. Originally a suburban meadow—the streets here bear names of indigenous flora and fauna—in the 17th century it was turned into a working-class neighborhood with rows of narrow canalfront homes. Artists and musicians have pioneered its recent renaissance, and now the yuppies have sniffed it out as well. The area has a high concentration of bars, cafes, restaurants, and clubs.

Etiquette

Closing time for most bars and cafes is 1am Monday through Thursday and Sunday, 2am on Friday and Saturday. Tipping isn't the social toll it is back home: Slide the bartender or waiter a guilder or two in appreciation, and then say *bedankt*.

The Lowdown

Brown cafes... Authenticity and goodwill resonate at Jordaan's **De Tuin**. Lace curtains bloom in the windows, and pockmarked wooden tables bear the sheen of years of elbows. It's a haunt of neighborhood shopkeepers, artists, and office workers who sit knee to knee until 1am, hoisting a *pils* or sipping cappuccino and ruminating about the nuances of modern life. Rather than regarding newcomers as poachers on sacred turf, Fobian, the owner of **Café de Nieuwe Lelie** regales them with stories of his annual pilgrimage to New Orleans. He willingly expounds on the Dutch custom of leaving two fingers of foam on the top of a beer and leveling the suds with a plastic knife—it's a Dutch thang. Fobian's bi-level corner bar in Jordaan is as comfortable as a faded pair of corduroys and as smoky as a hash den (although the only flammables inhaled here are legal). **Nota Bene**, a small bar just off Spui, verges on artsy, which could threaten its status as a neo-brown cafe. A tricycle hangs from the wall. A sound system the size of a NASA control panel projects jazz and funk throughout the bar. White candles leak suffused light. And the dartboard, precariously located near the front door, is always busy. The crowd is amiable and the bartenders impossibly good-looking. The 3am closing hour makes this a popular post-club, wind down spot.

Brown cafes worthy of Charles Bukowski... Raffish noir lighting makes silhouettes out of the crusty regulars entombed at the bar at **De Waag**. Too skanky for hoods and with a low-life factor sure to repel all yuppies who venture near, this smoke-choked, whiskey-swiller's haven near the Nieuwmarkt stays open until dawn. It could be a setting for a Tom Waits stream-of-scat song glorifying the down-and-out and the drinks they love. Dating from

THE BAR AND CAFE SCENE ◖ THE LOWDOWN

Central Amsterdam Bars

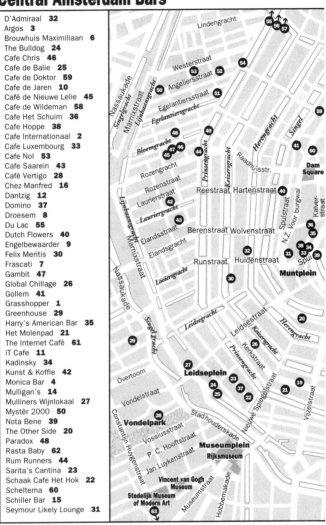

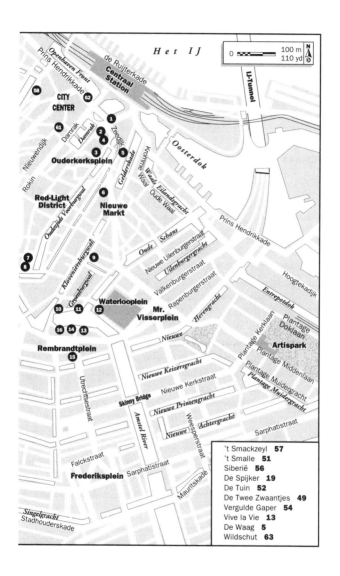

Het IJ

0   100 m
     110 yd

de Ruijterkade

Centraal
Station

IJ-Tunnel

Openhaven Front

Prins Hendrikkade

58   CITY
          CENTER   **62**

61   Damrak   Damrak   Zeedijk

1
2
4

3   **5**   Geldersekade

Ouderkerksplein

Oosterdok

Krommenwaal   Waals Eilandsgracht

Waal   Oude Waal

**Red-Light
District**

6

**Nieuwe
Markt**

Nieuwendijk

Rokin

Oudezijds Voorburgwal

Prins Hendrikkade

Oude   Schans

Oude   Nieuwe Uilenburgerstraat

Uilenburgergracht

7
8

9

Kloveniersburgwal

Groenburgwal

Valkenburgerstraat

Rapenburgerstraat

Hoogtekadijk

Entrepotdok

10   **11**   **12**

Waterlooplein

**Mr.
Visserplein**

Herengracht

Plantage
Doklaan

Plantage Kerklaan

Artispark

16   **14**   **13**

Nieuwe

Plantage Middenlaan

Rembrandtplein

15

Plantage Muidergracht

Plantage Muidergracht

Nieuwe Keizersgracht

Nieuwe Kerkstraat

Utrechtsestraat

Skinny Bridge

Nieuwe Prinsengracht

Nieuwe   Achtergracht

Amstel River

Sarphatistraat

Nieuwe   Weesperstraat

Falckstraat

Sarphatistraat

Frederiksplein

Mauritskade

Singelgracht
Stadhouderskade

't Smackzeyl	**57**
't Smalle	**51**
Siberië	**56**
De Spijker	**19**
De Tuin	**52**
De Twee Zwaantjes	**49**
Vergulde Gaper	**54**
Vive la Vie	**13**
De Waag	**5**
Wildschut	**63**

1624, **Cafe Chris** in Jordaan is Amsterdam's oldest bar, and some of the nightly patrons look as if they've been pickled and preserved since then. It's a mossy little place where locals seem startled whenever an unfamiliar face crosses the threshold. A grove of beer mugs hangs above a tiny bar; posters of Ajax, the local soccer team, curl off the walls; and a chalkboard lists regulars and their bar tabs. Oddly enough, on Sunday evenings the place takes on a "Masterpiece Theatre" kind of feel when opera broadcasts are piped in at maximum decibels.

Chess cafes... The Dutch call them *schaak* cafes—dens where tabletops are checkered and chess pieces vie for space with glasses of beer and ashtrays overflowing with butts. Traditionally, this is testosterone country where men gather to grunt and do a bit of board-dueling. **Gambit** in Jordaan is the quintessential representative of the genre. An oversized chessboard above the front door announces the game zone. Three steps down in the basement-level cafe, plants form green curtains against the front windows, timers tick like metronomes, and the smoke is thick enough to chew. **Schaak Cafe Het Hok** is anathema to the brassy, neon-buzzed restaurants, souvenir stands, and coffeeshops thickening the streets near the Leidseplein. It's as if the Yale Law Library were plunked into the midst of Coney Island. The decor is dingy—mismatched tables, scraggly carpeting, and a scrim of cigarette smoke. Though no regulations restrict women from entering, this chess cafe is understood as male turf. At **Domino** the games are backgammon, chess, and beer drinking, in that order. The competition is less intense than at most chess cafes. It feels like a college bar, complete with the smell of stale beer, yeasty armpits, and cigarette smoke so thick it could embroider the tattered chairs.

Where to drink waterside... The name of 't **Smalle** means "the narrow" in Dutch, and that aptly describes this 211-year-old, cramped two-story brown bar along Egelantiersgracht. Coziness is a given in this former distillery and tasting house. Red rosebushes crawl up the side of the pale yellow facade and canopy the doorway. Inside you're liable to encounter a herd of Japanese tourists, a drunken local ranting about the apocalypse, thirsty bohemians from the Jordaan environs, *and* a few KLM flight attendants celebrating a birthday, all competing to see which group can make the most noise. Benches and tables outside and across the street offer a more peaceful perch and afford bucolic views of gabled 17th-century canalhouses and passing boats. Housed in a former pharmacy, the **Vergulde Gaper** now dispenses libations to a decidedly yuppie crowd (fashion giveaways—blue blazers, braces, chinos, undershirts). Sawdust carpets the floor inside; tan and white awnings skirt the windows outside, where the real action is. Tables and wicker chairs line Prinsengracht and cluster on a small bridge crossing the canal. This is a good place to nurse a beer, muse on your good fortune, and scribble postcards home in the 10pm summer dusk. Guinness is on tap at **'t Smackzeyl** on Brouwersgracht, a brown cafe from central casting: a lively crowd in jeans, a welcoming atmosphere, and palpable mirth. A cafe as spacious as **Cafe de Jaren** is rare in this city of cozy spaces. Classified as a grand cafe, de Jaren's slick and spacious tiled interior and wide, two-story terrace overlooking the Amstel attracts lots of aesthetes and fashion victims.

Where margaritas rule... Connoisseurs of Mexico's most famous contribution to the world of cocktails won't be disappointed at **Sarita's,** where the bartenders mix fresh, mouth-puckering margaritas, rimming the glasses with orange juice to glue the salt in place. After you've shared a pitcher or two with your friends, move to a table and order one or two of Sarita's humongous burritos—the size of a loaf of bread—or go for a cholesterol special, an enchilada smothered in cheese. Frothy rum-based drinks and other pseudo-tropical libations are the draw at **Rum Runners**, a cavernous Jimmy Buffett-esque place tucked into the side courtyard of the Westerkerk. Occasional live music draws a twentysomething, backpacking crowd, but the Caribbean-based menu and the parade of cocktails—including a margarita that's a major contender—draw thirty- and fortysomethings as well.

Where to quaff Irish beer... Full-bodied, quenching, and satisfying, Dutch beer deserves copious praise and sampling. This being said, however, most big-time beer lovers would agree that Irish beer is brew you can chew.

Cafe Internationaal keeps British cider and Murphy's Irish Stout on tap. British expats park their glutes on the red bar stools coiled in a semicircle around the tiny bar and listen to Janis Joplin's raspy hits; things really kick into action after midnight, when the refugees from the nearby Red Light District tumble in. On weekend nights, tragically earnest Celtic bands play Irish folk music and drinking tunes at **Mulligan's**, the best of the flock of Irish bars in the city. The predictable cast of characters stalks this place—expats, Yeats fans, beer aficionados, and travelers with surnames like O'Leary, Ryan, Flannery, and Kelly. Guinness is on tap at the popular **'t Smackzeyl**, a brown cafe on the Brouwersgracht (Brewers' Canal) in Jordaan. The cacophony of voices conversing in English, Dutch, German, French, and a half dozen other languages tends to drown out the din of whatever is coming from the anemic jukebox.

Where to drink genever... Most of the *proeflokalen* are as small as a New York City studio apartment, but **D'Admiraal** is actually quite roomy. And whereas most are furnished with bar stools, D'Admiraal offers couches and overstuffed armchairs. It also stocks *genever* in dozens of incarnations from De Ooiyevaar, the city's only remaining independent distillery. The antiques that grace the brown interior at **Cafe de Doktor**, near Spui, are older than most of the patrons' great-grandparents. A stern armoire, ladder-back chairs, and chipped, ornamental plates give this place a clubby, New England feel. Though *proeflokalen* are typically the domain of guys who look like Norm on "Cheers," a younger crowd has recently started hanging out here. If you're worried you won't be able to stand up after downing a few shots of *genever* but you still want to sample it, go for brandied apricots, which are pickled in the stuff.

Strike a pose... The crowd at **Cafe Luxembourg** radiates the elusive incandescence of the In crowd (it's sort of an eerie, postnuclear glow). Popular for years with media, advertising, and assorted pinstriped types, this place has maintained its status as Amsterdam's ballast of hipness. High ceilings inside bespeak careless elegance. On Sunday nights, when much of the city is shuttered, Luxembourg is at full throttle, packed by those who want

to forestall another workweek. The back of the cafe over-
looks the Singel canal. Wearing black isn't a requirement
at **De IJsbreker**, but if you slouch in with running shoes
and a fanny pack, you'll probably feel like a shlump. The
cafe is appended to an international contemporary music
center (code for outré, atonal music center) that occasionally sponsors concerts as painful to endure as eating glass.
The cafe has a spectacular view of the Amstel; just ignore
the churlish Sprockets-types ruing the return of polyester
as a fashion force. The **Seymour Likely Lounge** could
have been plucked straight out of acknowledged First
World meccas of hipdom—South Beach, the Marais, or
Soho. Electric-colored plastic handbags dangle in rows in
the front window. The bold and the beautiful skitter
through the bar in three-day stubble or little black dresses. The lounge serves as a sort of appetizer for the hip
club of the same name across the street. Trendy but not
frosty, the youngish crowd favors cocktails over beer and
house music.

Where to meet the opposite sex... The area south of
the Heineken brewery is called De Pijp (the pipe) because
of its long, narrow streets (city planners apparently didn't
want to sacrifice precious living space for wide roadways).
Peopled by immigrants, artists, and young singles drawn
to cheaper rents, and site of the carnival-esque Albert
Cuypstraat flea market, this 'hood feels like Greenwich
Village in the late sixties. On the Roelof Hartplein square
in De Pijp, **Wildschut** boldly announces itself with a
green neon sign—a beacon for the hunters and the hunt-
ed. Thursday, Friday, and Saturday nights are for low-key
trolling in this neighborhood neo-brown cafe. The after-
work crowd loses its ties, jackets, pantyhose. People feed
guilders into the jukebox and scope the room, working
hard the whole time to quell any hint of desperation.
You'll have to wrestle with the decorations for a quiet corner in **Du Lac**. The interior resembles a prop shop after
an explosion, and the floor plan must have been drawn by
an architect on acid. Unexpected niches and alcoves invite
tête-à-têtes. An upstairs room, dominated by a circular
table and domed with a cupola, appears poised for a party
powwow. The backyard terrace is canopied with greenery
strung with green lights. On weekend nights hundreds of
singles—20s to 40s—turn this place into a mating

ground. **Frascati** is the name of a theater and cafe on Nes, a street known for experimental and fringe work—Amsterdam's Off-Off Broadway. Painted a regal purple inside, the cafe draws an assortment of theatergoers, most of them roué hipsters bent on death by smoking. Bring an oxygen mask or arrive before midnight if you want to avoid smoke so thick you could undress and nobody would notice. **Café Vertigo** is a buzzing, happening place on the terrace of the Netherlands Film Museum in Vondelpark, the largest swatch of greenery in the city center (Amsterdam's version of New York's Central Park). The moniker is an exaggeration; the sprawling, second-floor terrace does not induce nosebleeds or dizziness. Around 8pm each evening, the place is crowded enough to invite neighborly conversation with fellow people-watchers. By 10pm, the crowd has moved on.

Smoking coffeeshops... Hundreds of smoking coffeeshops are tucked into the neighborhoods of Amsterdam, but the award-winning **Greenhouse** stands out from the pack. Each year the judges of the Cannabis Cup Awards (the Pulitzer Prize of pot) shower this out-of-the-way coffeeshop with winner's cups and medals. A two-story enterprise, the top floor sports a couple of pool tables; downstairs are tables that provide better views of the mosaics gracing the interior. The smoking menu includes premier *nederweit* (home-grown weed) and the notorious, brain-paralyzing White Widow (a k a White Butterfly). A second branch, called **Greenhouse Namaste** (Nepali for "go in peace"), recently opened in the Waterlooplein area; it's worth making the pilgrimage if only to admire the phantasmagoric interior space, which seems to show the influences of Dali, the B-52s, and Jean-Michel Basquiat. The 4-foot-high hookah in the front window of **Kadinsky** says it all: Even though the place looks a little like a cozy salon, the amiable patrons are usually too cheesed on aromatic hashish to be able to engage in mind-fondling, salon-like discourse. **Rasta Baby** is Bob Marley territory, where everything is irie when you're buzzed on one of their particularly aromatic spliffs. Reggae pumps through the sound system and the shop serves booze, rare for a coffeeshop. The glassed-in front terrace feels like a terrarium on summer days. At **Dutch Flowers**, a small shop off Spui, the menu includes beer in addition to the staples: coffee, fruit juice, hashish, and marijuana (including some mighty fine skunk). The magazines, newspapers, and comic books are group property, though most times there's not that much reading going on since most of the herbally altered patrons seem to be distracted by the views of the Singel canal across the street. **Kunst & Koffie** delivers both "art and coffee," as its name promises. This Jordaan smoking shop squeezes art onto every inch of wall space. One of the grooviest puff shops in Jordaan, however, is **Siberië**, which also has a spate of portraiture, collages, and post-impressionist landscapes on the walls; the crowd here is a 50/50 locals/ tourists mix. The music runs to The Doors and Janis Joplin instead of the usual zombie-beat trance tunes or thump-insistent disco. The couches and oversized pillows make **Global Chillage** look like a rec room; the ambient music makes it sound like a dream sequence from some cheesy black-and-white movie back when women were called dames and men said "swelegant." The high-grade, moist hashish makes it all laughable, even the name. Droves of college students with backpacks regularly emerge from Centraal Station, walk a few paces down Damrak, and then veer toward **The Grasshopper**, a well-known waterfront smoking coffeeshop on the western fringes of the Red Light District. Then there's **The Bulldog**, the grand-daddy of 'em all. It's a chain store! It's a minimall! It's a corporate franchise!! (The chain even issued a cardboard coaster commemorating twenty years in the biz.) Bulldog has more branches in the city than McDonald's; you're bound to bump into one. But try to avoid the mother ship store on Leidseplein—it's way too loud and brassy.

Literary cafes... Where's Dorothy Parker when you need her? If the acerbic word-meister had ever haunted these city streets, she would undoubtedly have held court at **Engelbewaarder**, a louche cafe where writers and other intelligentsia mingle. The **Schiller Bar** on Rembrandt-plein is an oasis of elegance in a garish bouillabaisse of honky-tonk cafes, neon, and hordes of artless tourists. The art deco interior is enhanced by 1930s portraits of cabaret stars painted by the bar's namesake, Frits Schiller. Nostalgic for the gilded days before fast food and personal computers, the city's literati gather here for beer, cheer, and camaraderie. In the days before the Amsterdam 'burbs lured the daily papers out to the hinterlands, journalists working for *De Volkskrant* and *Amgemeen Dagblad* gathered at **Scheltema** to trade war stories. There are fewer journalists these days, but this brown cafe still has the same comfortable, rumpled feel and charged intellectual atmosphere it always had, thanks largely to a number of local literati, photographers, and artists spending their evenings here.

Culture-vulture cafes... **Frascati** on Nes, the avant-garde theater street, exudes the same sort of edginess engendered by ultraminimalist modern art. The cafe draws Sprockets devotees: black-clad, self-serious, wire-rimmed-spectacles types who patronize the Frascati Theater next door, a showcase for experimental works (a recent offering: an interpretative dance inspired by Jackson Pollock paintings and accompanied by atonal string music). A mirror the size of Montana sits behind the bar at Frascati, compounding the smug fabulousness radiating off everyone's face. Down several notches on the cool-o-meter, **Cafe de Balie** brooks no pretension. The gaudy parade of the Leidseplein unfurling outside the floor-to-ceiling windows is better than MTV. Inside is a crowd that eschews neon, nose rings, and noise. Patrons pore over earnest-sized hardcover books. A tableful of tourists grows silent over beers as they inscribe stacks of postcards. Habitués of the neighborhood's movie theaters trickle in, chattering about the films. Fringe theater bloomed at **Felix Meritis** in the late 1960s and early 1970s and there's still a whiff of the anything-goes days. Doric columns stand sentinel outside the gracefully proportioned 18th-century structure. The theater offers a no-surprises cultural menu—theater, video, seminars—but its reputation for dance performances is unshakable. The high-ceilinged cafe is a delicate and welcoming spot with a short menu of food and drinks. Next door to the architecturally clumsy and publicly reviled Stadhuis-Muziektheater (called Stopera by locals) is **Dantzig**, a grand cafe that imparts the elegance and Old World charm the Stopera snubs. Liveliest after performances, the cafe draws assorted crowds to the terrace skirting the Amstel and to the hushed interior, decorated with wooden library ladders and suffused uplighting beaming from the tops of decorative columns.

Where to find Dutch yuppies... They all talk on their cellular telephones at **Cafe Hoppe**, a perennially popular and trendy landmark (circa 1670) on Spui. They also all spend a lot of time fluffing their hair, adjusting their suspenders, and stretching to catch glimpses of themselves in the mirrors and windows. Of course, that's when they're not busy checking the stock market, bemoaning the high price of real estate, or trying to decide what to name their second child. More guppie (groovy urban professional) than yuppie, **Cafe Het Schuim** is part watering hole, part art gallery. The high walls double as exhibition space for local artists. Happy hour here belongs to students from the nearby university. During the evening shift, the thirtysomethings spill out onto the sidewalks. In a residential stretch of Prinsengracht flush with high-rent homes and apartment buildings but bereft of watering holes, the **Het Molenpad** is a welcome contender. Under a row of young trees that provide shade for some of the city's priciest real estate and just across the canal from a city public library, the narrow cafe's waterfront tables are chockablock when the sun makes a rare appearance and the temps climb. Provocative work—bold colors splashed on oversized canvases—adorns the interior walls. Billie Holiday croons on the tape deck. Solo visitors can park at the big reading table in the back of the room.

Where the boys are... The city's main gay zones are on Rembrandtplein, Kerkstraat, Reguliersdwarsstraat, and Warmoesstraat (fondly known by locals as La Rue de Vaseline). **Argos**, a hardcore pickup bar on Warmoesstraat, recalls the wincingly awful film *Cruising*, wherein Al Pacino trolled leather bars in search of something he didn't know he was looking for. Flinty-eyed muscle boys swaddled in leather and denim preen and cruise around the first-floor bar. Private cabins honeycomb the basement. The prevailing look is Nazi/cowboy/motorcycle cop—aim for anything worn by the Village People and you'll be jake. Dog collars are *de rigueur*. An ominous oversized spike impales the bar at **De Spijker**, a gay male hangout that also welcomes women and tourists. It's hard to tell what you'll find here. On some nights the bar lives up to its birthright as a fairly cruisy leather bar, on other nights the crowd includes visitors who look as if they just finished up dinner at Red Lobster and decided this might be a good place to

THE LOWDOWN ◡ THE BAR AND CAFE SCENE

wander in for a brewski (you can usually pick these tourists out—they're the ones trying to pretend they're *not* looking at the pornographic cartoons on the walls). The biggest gay scene on Saturday nights explodes at **iT**, a cavernous temple of homosexual bacchanalia (See The Club Scene). Across the street is the **iT Cafe**, a decidedly more low-key gathering spot for pre-club beers and dishing. Favored by gay men, the cafe welcomes straights and lesbians as well, but the loud, throbbing music forestalls conversation and encourages lipreading. Maybe that's the idea. **The Other Side** (the "other side" is a Dutch euphemism for being gay) is a smoking coffeeshop close to the premier gay nightclubs Havana and April's Exit (see The Club Scene). The boys drop in here for something from the small hash menu, a shot of espresso, or a toke or two. The soundtrack is high-decibel disco.

Where the girls are... There's no real lesbian-only night-club scene to speak of. Instead, one-night parties rotate among various venues, advertised in several publications like *Trash in the Streets*, a free, twice-monthly gay and lesbian newspaper and *Ma'dam*, a monthly lesbian magazine. Lesbians of all stripes, ranging in age from early 20s to sixtysomething, do gather at **Cafe Saarein**, the only hangout in town exclusively for women. No men, period. A brown cafe in Jordaan, Cafe Saarein is a low-key place with a billiards table, decor reminiscent of Aunt Minnie's parlor, oversized windows for women-watching among the passersby, and a bulletin board where lesbian parties are announced. The bartenders are usually a good source of information about other lesbian happenings around town. Just off gaudy Rembrandtplein, **Vive la Vie** is pre-dominantly a women's hangout, though the crowd usually includes a smattering of straights and gay men. For the most part, this is lipstick lesbian territory—femme posses decked in skirts and boots lean alluringly against the small bar, while coy couples huddle around the tables, hands fluttering gently over each other's thighs and newly styled coifs. **Monica Bar**, home of butch lesbionics, is a small, dark, semi-cruisy dive populated primarily by women who favor short hair, baggy paramilitary garb, and multiple silver hoops in their ears. A few lipstick les-bians and straight women dolly up the place a bit, but the testosterone set is barred from entry.

For camp and color… Zsa Zsa Gabor and Liberace must have done the interior of **Cafe Nol**, a thoroughly kitsch sing-along bar in Jordaan. It's a drag queen's wet dream: the windows are framed in hot-pink neon and a half dozen mini-chandeliers dangle above the fringe-trimmed bar. Velvet-tufted stools encircle tables lit from beneath— they look a little like futuristic space pods. Insouciant cherubs dangle from the ceiling. The music is of the blustery, Dutch oompah-pah variety, and, after they've had enough liquid encouragement, patrons sidle up to the karaoke machine and let it rip. Within stumbling distance of Cafe Nol, **De Twee Zwaantjes** is smaller, more raucous, and blessed (burdened?) with its own accordion player. You may not be able to sing along with the Jordaan locals as they warble and gargle their way through Dutch folk songs, but who cares? Beer helps crumble international barriers, and in this neighborhood joint, much tippling is mandatory. It's frequented by the dentally challenged, the exuberantly looped, and the musically uplifted (if not talented). Named after local club-meister Manfred Langer (who also owns the gay iT and iT Cafe), **Chez Manfred**, a rowdy, kitschy sing-along pub close to Rembrandtplein, one of the city's gay zones, is impossibly crowded and infectiously friendly. On most evenings it's patronized by a mix of campy gays and straights. Local demi-celeb and drag queen Nicky Nicole and her entourage sweep through periodically.

Juice bars… Like free love, jumbo shrimp, and military intelligence, a smokeshop juice bar seems an oxymoron, yet it exists at **Paradox**. The menu is organic food in the guise of smoothies, salads, and fruit-veggie juice combos, alongside combustible euphorics in the form of hashish and skunk. If you're feeling daring, you might want to try the Pan Galactic Gargle Blaster, which bears the name of Douglas Adams's sci-fi über-alcoholic beverage but is actually an organic tonic of fresh vegetable juices. Though she might have had problems with all the smoking, the food would actually have passed muster with Adele Davis. The crowd leans heavily toward affable expats.

Wine bars… Opening a wine bar in the city crossed by the Amstel river is seen by many locals as a breach of decorum, if not an outright act of treason. True wine bars are scarcer than cowboy boots in these parts. Nevertheless, a few adventurous proprietors are boldly going where no Amsterdammers have gone before: **Droesem** bills itself as the city's first real wine cafe. Overall, it's a dignified, adult sort of place, though barrels of wine lend a rustic air. Delicatessen-style noshes include platters of cheese, fish, and meat. Both the (unspoken) dress code and the decor at **Mulliners Wijnlokaal** elicit adjectives like tony, upmarket, polished. More than six dozen wines grace the menu. Candles perch on tabletops and classical tunes waft through the air, prompting spontaneous romantic gestures.

Online cafes... Surf's up in Amsterdam, even though it's a beachless city striped with polluted canals. Insiders say the city is behind the curve when it comes to interest in the Internet, but anyone twitching for a cyberfix, suffering from E-mail withdrawal, or hungering to surf the Net can duck into **Internet Café** and have all those technological needs met. One-stop shopping for all of life's essential food groups: hash, espresso, and the World Wide Web. Park at one of the computers for Dfl 10 an hour. It's staffed by ardent computer nerds who are exceedingly patient with technophobes. **Mystèr 2000**, a self-consciously nineties multimedia cybercenter located in a former Jordaan textile factory, has performance space, library, exhibition area, smart bar, computer center. On Thursday, Internet night, travelers can retrieve E-mail, check the weather in Ulan Bator, or research Peru's three principal exports on the dozen computers.

Beer bars... It wouldn't be an exaggeration to call **Cafe de Wildeman** a temple to beer. The tap heads of about two dozen draft beers poke above the bar like a cluster of emaciated bowling pins, and more than two hundred bottled beers—mostly potent Euro-brands—are on hand as well. Bowls of salted munchies like peanuts, pretzels, and cheesy little cracker bits help keep the beer-swilling patrons thirsty. Beer fanatics of every national stripe are drawn here like homing pigeons, and the din is mezzo forte. At **Gollem**, the regulars have developed the beer-drinking equivalent of tennis elbow. Claustrophobics will be on red-alert in this tiniest of bars with happy hour and early evening crowds that grow exponentially and take over the sidewalk outside. A bit off the beaten track but well worth the journey is the **Bierbrouwerij 't IJ**, a microbrewery housed in the Funenkade *molen* (windmill). Tattooed with graffiti throughout, this funky spot is definitely *not* dressed to impress. Though the bar is only open Wednesday through Sunday until 8:30pm, pilgrims flock to this photoworthy mecca to drink the lethal home brews (some have 12 percent alcohol content); a favorite is the russet-colored Columbus. When the weather is warm, the terrace fills up with the tank-top-and-shorts crowd, faces tilted skyward. **Brouwhuis Maximiliaan** is the city's other microbrewery. Parked in a seedier neighborhood near the Red Light District, it attracts younger locals who come to pay homage to the high-octane home brew.

Where to drink a martini... Spuistraat is the address of some of the city's enduringly popular cafes, most thronged with people who look like advertisements for the Good Life. **Harry's American Bar** is not one of those places, however. Instead, languorous jazz tapes, heavy on the sax, provide the sound track for a gathering of patrons who look like retired university professors. The draw here is the bar's resolute non-grooviness and its list of lethal cocktails. The Dfl 9 martini is a deceptively smooth potion with the requisite one-two punch.

THE LOWDOWN ⟨ THE BAR AND CAFE SCENE

The Index

Closing hours for most bars and cafes are 1am Sun–Thur and 2am Fri–Sat; exceptions are noted. No credit cards are accepted unless otherwise noted.

D'Admiraal. A quintessential *proeflokaal* (tasting house for Dutch gin) with an outdoor patio.... *Tel 020/624-8443. Herengracht 319, tram 13 or 17. Closed Sun.*

Argos. Landmark bar in the city's gay leather district. Cruise central, private cabins, and men only.... *Tel 020/622-6595. Warmoesstraat 95; tram 4, 9, 16, 24, or 25. Open until 3am Mon–Thur, until 4am Fri and Sat.*

Bierbrouwerij 't IJ. Housed in one of Amsterdam's six windmills, this bar has its own brewery and label (request a Columbus, a potent, medium-dark brew).... *Tel 020/ 622-8325. Funenkade 7, tram 6 or 10. Open Wed–Sun until 8:30pm.*

Brouwhuis Maximiliaan. One of the city's two microbreweries. Near the Red Light District, this microbrewery draws a younger crowd than the other one.... *Tel 020/ 624-2778. Kloveniersburgwal 6-8, Metro Nieuwmarkt. Closed Sun and Mon.*

The Bulldog. Kind of like an herbal McDonald's, branches of this 20-year-old smoking coffeeshop are scattered around town—there are three in the same block of the Red Light District. The mother ship store/bar/cafe graces Leidseplein.... *Tel 020/627-1908. Leidseplein 15; tram 1, 2, 5, 6, 7, 10, or 11. Open daily.*

Cafe Chris. On Sunday evenings, when opera is broadcast at heart-stirring decibels, a culture-vulture crowd fills this

Jordaan neighborhood dive bar/cafe .... *Tel 020/624–5942. Bloemstraat 42; tram 13, 14, or 17. Open daily until 3am.*

Cafe de Balie. Just off the hubbub of Leidseplein, the high ceilings and oversized windows of this low-key place create a soothing space for mellowing out, daydreaming, regrouping.... *Tel 020/624–9088. Kleine Garmanplantsoen 10; tram 6, 7, or 10. Open daily.*

Cafe de Doktor. The prescription in this inviting tasting house is Dutch gin and brandied fruit.... *No telephone. Rozenboomsteg 4; tram 1, 2, 5, or 11. Closed Sun.*

Cafe de Jaren. An appealingly trendy two-story cafe with a spacious, classy interior of pastel tile, oversized modern art, and high-tech lighting. Two outdoor terraces overlook the Amstel River.... *Tel 020/625–5771. Nieuwe Doelenstaat 20; tram 4, 9, 14, 16, 24, or 25. Closed Mon. Major credit cards accepted.*

Café de Nieuwe Lelie. Hush Puppie–comfy brown cafe in Jordaan run by amiable Fobian, who looks like a founding member of ZZ Top.... *Tel 020/622–5493. Nieuwe Leliestraat 83; tram 10, 13, 14, or 17. Closed Sun.*

Cafe de Wildeman. The quintessential beer bar, with more than 250 bottled brews stored in the cellar and up to 2 dozen on tap. Expat haven as well as a local hangout.... *Tel 020/638–2348. Nieuwezijds Kolk 3; tram 4, 9, 14, 24, or 25. Closed Sun.*

Cafe Het Schuim. An über-cool, see-and-be-seen cafe filled with university students and representatives of life's more creative subcultures.... *Tel 020/638–9357. Spuistraat 189; tram 1, 5, or 11. Open daily.*

Cafe Hoppe. A city landmark dating from 1670 and one of the most popular happy-hour bars with the briefcase-on-bicycles crowd.... *Tel 020/623–7849. Spui 18–20; tram 1, 2, 4, 5, 9, 11, 16, 24, or 25. Open daily.*

Cafe Internationaal. Brown cafe near the Red Light District frequented by British expats with a hankering for cider and

THE INDEX

THE BAR AND CAFE SCENE

Murphy's Irish Stout (the cappuccino of beers) on tap.... *Tel 020/624–5520. Warmoesstraat 1; tram 4, 9, 16, 20, 24, or 25. Open daily until 4am.*

Cafe Luxembourg. Yuppie mecca for the business and media crowd and the place to be on Sunday night.... *Tel 020/ 620–6264. Spuistraat 22; tram 1, 2, 5, 11, 13, or 17. Open daily. Major credit cards accepted.*

Cafe Nol. High-camp karaoke bar where locals sing Dutch drinking songs amidst fringes, cherubs, chandeliers, and pink neon.... *Tel 020/624–5380. Westerstraat 109; tram 13, 14, or 17. Open daily until 3am.*

Cafe Saarein. Small, elegant, Jordaan brown cafe for women only.... *Tel 020/623–4901. Elandsstraat 119, tram 7 or 10. Closed Sun.*

Café Vertigo. Hip central, bi-level outdoor cafe on the terrace of the film museum in Vondelpark. Greenery, water, and a street carnival below.... *Tel 020/612–3021. Nederlands Filmmuseum, Vondelpark 3; tram 1, 2, 3, 5, 6, 11, or 12. Open daily.*

Chez Manfred. Sodden sing-along bar frequented by drag queens, fey gay men, and all who clamor to whirl in the lighthearted hijinks.... *Tel 020/626–4510. Halvermaansteeg 10; tram 4, 9, or 14. Open daily.*

Dantzig. Located next to the Stadhuis-Muziektheater, this a fave spot for a post-performance and/or post-prandial libation.... *Tel 020/620–9039. Zwanenburgwal 15; tram 9 or 14, Metro Waterlooplein. Open daily. Major credit cards accepted.*

Domino. Smoky chess cafe frequented by a loyal group of (predominantly male) regulars.... *No telephone. Leidsekruistraat 19; tram 1, 2, 5, 6, 7, 10, or 11. Closed Sun.*

Droesem. One of the city's few wine bars. Barrels of several of the establishment's favorite vintages add warmth to the decor, and artfully presented cheese platters satisfy the munchies.... *Tel 020/620–3316. Nes 41; tram 4, 9, 14, 16, 24, or 25. Open daily.*

Du Lac. Regal-gothic kitsch decor is splashed over every visible inch of this popular singles cafe. Semi-hidden niches, private rooms, and a small terrace under a canopy of trees sprinkled with green Christmas lights.... *Tel 020/ 624–4265. Haarlemmerstraat 11; bus 18, 22, or 44. Closed Sun.*

Dutch Flowers. A city center smoking coffeeshop that sells a healthy variety of decently priced hashish and serves beer (a rarity in smokehouses).... *Tel 020/624–7624; Singel 387; tram 1, 2, 5, or 11. Open daily.*

Engelbewaarder. The cafe voted most likely to become the site of Amsterdam's Algonquin roundtable. Rife with writers, students, and poets and abuzz with literary conversation.... *Tel 020/625–3772. Kloveniersburgwal 59; tram 4, 9, or 14; Metro Nieuwmarkt. Open daily.*

Felix Meritis. An airy bar and cafe in a classically designed, historical building of the same name (translation: "Deservingly Happy"), now site of Amsterdam Summer University.... *Tel 020/623–1311. Keizersgracht 324; tram 13, 14, or 17. Open Tues–Sat until 10pm.*

Frascati. Ebullient theater bar in the midst of Amsterdam's Off-Off Broadway district.... *Tel 020/624–1324. Nes 59; tram 4, 9, 14, 16, 24, or 25. Open daily.*

Gambit. A scruffy Jordaan chess bar announced by the board hanging outside the door.... *No telephone. Bloemgracht 20; tram 13, 14, or 17. Open daily.*

Global Chillage. Smoking coffeeshop higher up on decor food chain than the rest. Ambient music, overstuffed couches and chairs, muted lighting, and woody, sweet hash smoke billowing into a smoky scrim.....*Tel 020/639–1154. Kerkstraat 51; tram 1, 2, 5, or 11. Open until midnight daily.*

Gollem. Beer central, with dozens of varieties and an amiable crowd. A good pre-dinner stop.... *Tel 020/626–6645. Raamsteeg 4; tram 1, 2, 5, or 11. Open daily.*

Grasshopper. This smoking coffeeshop inches from Centraal Station is a stopping point for every backpacker who hits the city.... *Tel 020/626–1529. Oudebrugsteeg 16; tram 4, 9, 16, 24, or 25. Open daily.*

Greenhouse. This smoking coffeeshop is a perennial award-winner in the annual Cannabis Cup competition, both for its interior decor and for the quality of the herbs for sale.... *Tel 020/673–7430. Tollenstraat 91, tram 7 or 17. Open daily.*

Harry's American Bar. Scratchy jazz soundtrack, older patrons, brown cafe interior, and a lethal list of cocktails.... *Tel 020/624–4384. Spuistraat 285; tram 1, 2, 5, or 11. Closed Sun.*

Het Molenpad. Popular, preppy bar and dinner spot with over-sized reading table, outstanding cafe grub, and palpable convivial atmosphere.... *Tel 020/625–9680. Prinsengracht 653; tram 1, 2, 5, 7, or 11. Open daily.*

De IJsbreker. This bar adjoining a contemporary music center is a magnet for moody artistes sporting asymmetrical hair-cuts; black is the (only) clothing color of choice.... *Tel 020/668–1805. Weesperzijde 23; tram 3, 6, 7, or 10. Open daily.*

The Internet Café. A 5-minute walk from Centraal Station. Music, on-line surfing, hashish, drinks, and mellow cyber-vibes.... *Tel 020/620–0902; Nieuwendijk 30; tram 1, 2, 4, 5, 9, 13, 14, 16, 17, 24, or 25. Closed Sun.*

iT Cafe. Low-key gay bar across the street from the frantic and popular club of the same name....*Tel 020/420–0935. Amstelstraat 27; tram 4, 9, or 14. Open daily until 3am.*

Kadinsky. Comfy, smoky, hazy smoking coffeeshop off Spui.... *Tel 020/624–7023. Rosmarijnsteeg 9; tram 1, 2, 4, 5, 9, 11, 14, 16, 24, or 25. Open daily.*

Kunst & Koffie. With its wall space adorned by works of local artists, this Jordaan smoking coffeeshop is an aesthetic cut above the norm.... *Tel 020/622–5960. Tweede Laurier-dwarsstraat 64; tram 13, 14, or 17. Closed Sun.*

Monica Bar. A Red Light District lesbian bar that's a lot more butch than femme. Women only.... *No telephone.*

Lange Neizel 15; tram 4, 9, 16, 24, or 25. Closed Sun and Mon.

Mulligan's. The heartiest of the Irish bars in town. Live music Wed–Sat and the requisite cast of sodden, misunderstood poets, ne'er-do-wells, and expats suffering from Guinness withdrawal.... *Tel 020/622–1330. Amstel 100; tram 4, 9, or 14. Open daily.*

Mulliners Wijnlokaal. One of the city's few wine bars, this one is amiable and affordable and serves good food.... *No telephone. Lijnbaansgracht 267; tram 6, 7, or 10. Open daily.*

Mystèr 2000. Housed in a former textile factory, this cyber-center has a bar, performance space, and library. Thursday night patrons can surf the Net or send E-mail.... *Tel 020/ 620–2970. Lijnbaansgracht 92. Open daily, Thur until midnight. Dfl 15 per hour for computer use.*

Nota Bene. A primo post-club stop for a beer and a wee bit more conviviality.... *Tel 020/624–7461. Voerboogstraat 4; tram 1, 2, 5, or 11. Open daily.*

The Other Side. One of a handful of gay smoking coffeeshops in the heart of the Reguliersdwarsstraat gay ghetto.... *Tel 020/625–5141. Reguliersdwarsstraat 6; tram 1, 2, 5, or 11. Open daily.*

Paradox. Cozy smoking coffeeshop favored by slumming Sloane Ranger-types; a vegetarian menu a cut above the coffee-shop norm. The fruit shakes satisfy herbally induced munchies.... *Tel 020/623–5639. 1e Bloemdwarsstraat 2; tram 13, 14, or 17. Open daily.*

Rasta Baby. Bob Marley and his ilk have hijacked the sound system in this smoking coffeeshop just a spliff's toss away from Centraal Station. Cop a seat in the glass-enclosed terrace.... *Tel 020/624–7403. Prins Hendrikkade 6–7; tram 1, 2, 4, 5, 9, 11, 13, 16, 17, 24, or 25. Open daily.*

Rum Runners. Lethal cocktails, Hawaiian-shirt crowd, and frat-boy ambience.... *Tel 020/627–4079. Prinsengracht 277; tram 13 or 17. Open daily. Major credit cards accepted.*

THE INDEX

THE BAR AND CAFE SCENE

Sarita's Cantina. This well-stocked cocktail bar mixes a mean margarita and draws a lively weekend crowd.... *Tel 020/ 627–7840; Lange Leidsedwarsstraat 29; tram 1, 2, 5, 11, 13, or 17. Open daily.*

Schaak Cafe Het Hok. Earnest chess cafe with earnest men smoking earnest cigarettes contemplating their next earnest maneuver.... *Tel 020/624–3133. Lange Leidse-dwarsstraat 134; tram 1, 2, 5, or 11. Open daily.*

Scheltema. Known citywide as a journalists/literati watering hole. Best early in the evening for cocktails.... *Tel 020/ 623–2323. Nieuwezijds Voorburgwal 212; tram 1, 2, 5, 11, 13, or 17. Open Mon–Fri until 11pm, Sat and Sun until 9pm.*

Schiller Bar. Art nouveau grandeur and a hushed elegance amidst the garish, neon scream of Rembrandtplein.... *Tel 020/624–9846. Rembrandtplein 26; tram 4, 19, or 14. Open daily.*

Seymour Likely Lounge. No scruffiness tolerated in this trend-o-matic pomo bar across from red-hot club of same name.... *Tel 020/627–1427. Nieuwezijds Voorburgwal 250; tram 1, 2, 5, or 11. Open daily. Major credit cards accepted.*

't Smackzeyl. A brown cafe scoring big points for location, location, location. Large windows overlook the city's 2 most attractive waterways—the exceedingly bucolic Brouwersgracht and the Prinsengracht.... *Tel 020/622–6520. Brouwersgracht 101; tram 1, 2, 5, 11, 13, or 17. Open daily.*

't Smalle. This little wedge of a brown cafe in the Jordaan is always lively and the apogee of the picturesque brown cafe.... *Tel 020/623–9617. Egelantiersgracht 12, tram 13, 14, 17. Open until 1am.*

Siberië. Proximity to Centraal Station, music by The Doors, and consistently high-quality herbal products make this smoking coffeeshop a checkpoint for backpackers and locals.... *Tel 020/623–5909. Brouwersgracht 11, tram 3 or 10. Open daily.*

De Spijker. Gay leather cruise bar with porno cartoons twitching on the walls and a huge, self-referential spike (*de spijker*) on the bar.... *Tel 020/620–5919. Kerkstraat 4; tram 1, 2, 5, or 11. Open daily.*

De Tuin. Jordaan brown bar popular with life's fringe-dwellers bent on conversation.... *Tel 020/624–4559. Tweede Tuin-dwarsstraat 13; tram 3, 10, 13, 14, or 17. Open daily.*

De Twee Zwaantjes. Sliver of a bar in Jordaan where the norm is beer guzzling and yodeling to campy accordian music.... *Tel 020/625–2729. Prinsengracht 114; tram 13, 14, or 17. Open daily.*

Vergulde Gaper. Popular and unpretentious Jordaan bar with a heated terrace and dozens of coveted outdoor tables along the Prinsengracht.... *Tel 020/624–8975. Prinsengracht 30, tram 3 or 10. Open daily.*

Vive la Vie. Lipstick lesbian bar as noisy as Rembrandtplein outside. Men welcome.... *Tel 020/624–0114. Amstelstraat 7; tram 4, 9, or 14. Closed Sun.*

De Waag. Neighborhood dive where the surly patrons look askance at any sign of chirpiness.... *Tel 020/624–6449. Zeedijk 130, Metro Nieuwmarkt or Centraal Station. Open until 6am daily.*

Wildschut. Comfy, clubby cafe with outdoor terrace and thickets of happy hour business types. An in spot for thirtysome-things.... *Tel 020/676–8220. Roelof Hartplein 1–3; tram 3, 5, 12, 24, or 25. Open daily.*

THE BAR AND CAFE SCENE / THE INDEX

the

3

arts

Dutch audiences hold fast
to the "Star Trek"
manifesto: They want to
boldly go where no
audience has gone before.
What applies in the
U.S. to government—

of the people, by the people, and for the people—here refers to the arts. Enthusiastic audience support has helped modern dance in Amsterdam, for example, become Europe's best. Even the Dutch government likes art. Though subsidies have dropped off, performers here benefit from wide-eyed support and can live off the fat of the land.

Dutch Masters? Van Gogh? Rembrandt? For centuries, Amsterdammers have been weaned on a steady diet of painting as well as dance and music. Nationwide, you'll find a museum for every 15 square miles, making Holland the country with the highest concentration of museums in the world. (Unfortunately, few are open at night.) More than 250 galleries dot the city's streets. From futuristic techno noise, to jazz quintets, to an organ concert in one of the city's churches, the city's musical menu has something for everybody. Free art abounds, thanks to street painter's murals splashed across squatted buildings and people like the saxophonist who plays in the evenings beneath the Rijksmuseum. The dance and music scenes have a steady succession of newcomers.

Since the end of World War II, the Dutch government has provided generous subsidies to individual artists and to performing groups, enabling survival and experimentation— but also, critics say, far too much navel-gazing and self-indulgence. The Netherlands, and Amsterdam in particular, became known as one of the few places in Europe where government helped artists. Eastern European, Pacific Rim, and African artists made their pilgrimages here, hoping for a meal courtesy of the government. By the mid-eighties, there were more than 4,000 artists receiving some sort of support. All good things come to an end, however. By the start of the nineties, largesse dwindled and the generous arts program was discontinued. (Governmental arts subsidies continue today, but on a much smaller scale.) Theater, opera, and ballet grew conservative— by Dutch standards. As fringe groups faded away, safe classics were trotted out and performed to ensure audiences and ticket sales. Arts groups turned to corporate and industry sponsorship to help foot their bills. Where else does the national philharmonic partner with AGA and a Japanese health food manufacturer? Once financial footing was regained, Dutch audiences again got what they wanted: innovation.

Opera had never been a Dutch forté. But it became a hot ticket in town in the early nineties after the new artistic director Pierre Audi staged productions that wouldn't see light in Milan or Bayreuth. He imported the elliptical, arty British filmmaker Peter Greenaway (*The Cook, the Thief, His Wife, and*

Her Lover) to collaborate with composer Louis Andriessen, resulting in Greenaway's first opera libretto, *Rosa*. You can still find the likes of *Swan Lake*, *A Comedy of Errors*, or *Madama Butterfly* on city playbills, but the productions are flashier and slicker than those standards in London, New York, or Paris. Ticket prices for an evenings of opera or ballet are usually less than Dfl 100, which makes this European capital one of the cheapest places to see first-rate performances.

In summer, Amsterdam goes al fresco, with performances in the city's streets, parks, squares, and open-air theaters, drawing large crowds during long days that don't end until 10pm. Smart move, considering that most Amsterdammers wouldn't trade a rare moment of sunshine to step inside and watch tutus twirl. The **Holland Festival** transpires during June, showcasing theater, dance, and music both indoors and out. During the entire summer, the outdoor **Over het IJ Festival** is marked by large-scale experimental works in dance, theater, movement, and music. Capping the summer is **Uitmarkt**, a weekend outdoor festival wherein local dance, music, and theater companies preview their upcoming seasons in a series of free, performances. And the seasonal finale to the arts smorgasbord is the annual, free outdoor performance sponsored by the Pulitzer Hotel on Prinsengracht. During the twilight hours, a symphony orchestra plays from a barge moored in the canal in front of the hotel. Hundreds make the pilgrimage with chairs, picnic baskets, and blankets.

Getting Tickets

Major classical performances in dance, opera, and music are likely to be sold out weeks in advance. Lesser known companies perform at smaller venues where fewer seats and tickets are available. It is best to book tickets immediately and *not* wait for the day of the show. And don't count on scalping; it's just not done here. But do bear in mind that for several venues, including the neoclassical music hall Concertgebouw, ticket prices are lower for Monday through Thursday performances. The nexus for booking and for arts info is the **AUB** (Amsterdam Uitburo), located beside the Stadschouwburg in Leidseplein. You can also book directly from the venue or through the **VVV** for a small service charge (see Down and Dirty). To make reservations from the states, before you travel, call the VVV or a Netherlands Tourism Board in the states. The invaluable printed source of arts info is *Uitkrant*, a free monthly listings magazine printed in Dutch, but easy to understand.

82

Central Amsterdam Arts

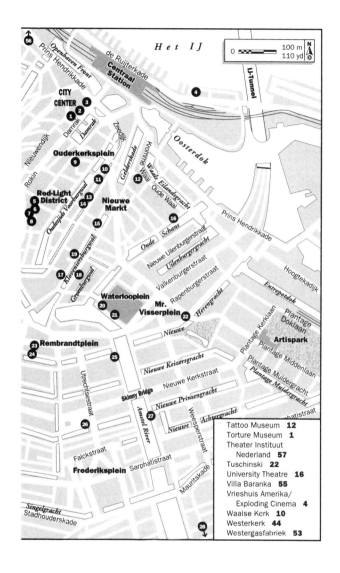

Het IJ

0   100 m
      110 yd

N

IJ-Tunnel

Openhaven Front

Prins Hendrikkade

de Ruijterkade

Centraal
Station

CITY
CENTER

Damrak

Damrak

Zeedijk

Nieuwendijk

Ouderkerksplein

Oosterdok

Kromme Waal

Waals Eilandsgracht

Oude Waal

Gelderskade

Rokin

Red-Light
District

Oudezijds Voorburgwal

Nieuwe
Markt

Oude Schans

Nieuwe Uilenburgerstraat

Uilenburgergracht

Prins Hendrikkade

Kloveniersburgwal

Groenburgwal

Uilenburgerstraat

Valkenburgerstraat

Rapenburgerstraat

Hoogtekadijk

Entrepotdok

Waterlooplein

Mr.
Visserplein

Herengracht

Nieuwe

Plantage
Doklaan

Plantage Kerklaan

Artispark

Rembrandtplein

Plantage Middenlaan

Plantage Muiderlaan

Nieuwe Keizersgracht

Nieuwe Kerkstraat

Plantage Muidergracht

Plantage Muidergracht

Skinny Bridge

Amstel River

Nieuwe Prinsengracht

Utrechtsestraat

Nieuwe Weesperstraat

Nieuwe Achtergracht

...hatistraat

Falckstraat

Weesperstraat

Frederiksplein

Sarphatistraat

Mauritskade

Singelgracht

Stadhouderskade

Tattoo Museum	**12**
Torture Museum	**1**
Theater Instituut Nederland	**57**
Tuschinski	**22**
University Theatre	**16**
Villa Baranka	**55**
Vrieshuis Amerika/ Exploding Cinema	**4**
Waalse Kerk	**10**
Westerkerk	**44**
Westergasfabriek	**53**

The Arts in the Museumplein Area & Amsterdam South

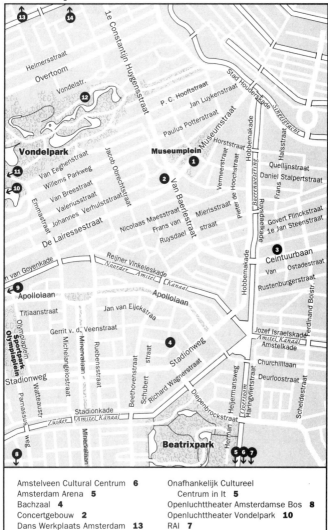

Amstelveen Cultural Centrum **6**
Amsterdam Arena **5**
Bachzaal **4**
Concertgebouw **2**
Dans Werkplaats Amsterdam **13**
Netherlands Filmmuseum **12**
OCCII **11**

Onafhankelijk Cultureel
 Centrum in It **5**
Openluchttheater Amsterdamse Bos **8**
Openluchttheater Vondelpark **10**
RAI **7**
Ravensbrück Monument **1**
Rialto **3**

The Arts in Amsterdam East

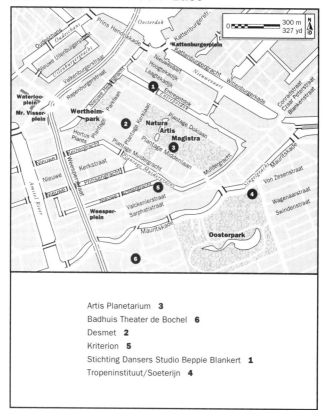

Artis Planetarium **3**

Badhuis Theater de Bochel **6**

Desmet **2**

Kriterion **5**

Stichting Dansers Studio Beppie Blankert **1**

Tropeninstituut/Soeterijn **4**

The Lowdown

Where it's at... Politics and opera do a strange tango in Amsterdam; both are housed in the **Muziektheater**, known locally as the "Stopera," a combo of State House and Opera House. The nickname is an acidic shorthand for "Stop the Opera," a protest against the cohabitation of government and music, and the destruction of historic homes mowed over to clear the riverfront site. If awards were given out for "Most Controversial Contemporary Building," the Stopera would be Amsterdam's unaninmous winner. Hailed by one composer as a "monument of mediocrity and lack of taste," the building has been the subject of bashing since 1954 when Waterlooplein—a seedy neighborhood—was chosen as its site. The plan called for the destruction of more than three dozen medieval houses, which were at the heart of the city's Middle Ages Jewish quarter. The project lay in limbo for 25 years until it was decided to make arts and government unlikely bedfellows. That move riled locals as did the out-of-place, grimly modern architecture. Architects Wilhelm Holtzbauer and Cees Dam's white marble, red brick, and glass crescent prompted demonstrations and vandalism during construction in 1982 that caused more than a million guilders in damage. The 1,600-seat building is airy (some say arid) and houses the Nederlandse Opera (see "What's opera, doc?" below) and the Nationale Ballet (see "Men in tights, women in tutus," below). It also boasts dramatic, sweeping views of the Amstel.

By contrast, Amsterdam's municipal drama theater, the **Stadsschouwburg**, is the most exquisite venue in the city. It is the third successive incarnation on the same site; the first two buildings were destroyed by fire. The resident theater company, Toneelgroep, performs only in Dutch, so English speakers who want to see the interior usually opt for a dance performance or one of the architectural tours. Plush red carpets line the floors of the horseshoe-shaped building, which, with its baroque detailing, balconies, and ornate trims, looks like a slice of wedding cake. A small adjunct space called **Bovenzaal** hosts pared-down productions—dance, theater, and musical—that wouldn't be able to fill the larger theater. Even if you can't score tickets to a show, make time to at least swing by the cafe for a cup of espresso and a chance to ogle the interior. The innovative and envelope-pushing music presented by **De IJsbreker** is thoroughly modern. The name—"the icebreaker"—may now be understood as a nod to the center's innovative programming, but it actually has more prosaic origins in Dutch history. In the 17th century, a group of men braved the brutal winter to break the ice at this site to create safe passage for merchant ships. Today, a streamlined contemporary building overlooking the Amstel hosts an eclectic modern music series. If you want indigenous people plucking hand harps or atonal works by Dutch composers, come here. It's also a site for Holland Festival concerts every June. The people-watching alone make this place worth the price of admission: angular haircuts, scruffy but stylish shoes, wire-rim spectacles, the tendency to exhale earnestly. It's a crowd that takes *Art Forum* and Baudrillard to heart.

If architecture elevates the pulse at all, the **Beurs van Berlage** on the Damrak can induce arrythmia. Home of the **Nederlands Philharmonisch Orkest** (tel 020/627-0466), the quietly fabulous 1903 building once housed the city stock exchange and is the showpiece of Amsterdam School-pater Hendrik Berlage. Quite simply, you'll be stunned by the building's color and whimsy. The facade is laced with blue, gold, rust, and white brick rimming the archways. The two halls have unabashedly adopted the names of the corporate sugar daddies who ponied up big money to sponsor the arts and renovate the building. *AGA Zaal* honors the the gas company, while *Wang Zaal* pays tribute to the computer company who withdrew sponsorship due to financial woes. (Though a Japanese health food drink manufacturer stepped in with ample bucks, the hall still bears the computer company's moniker.) Just south of the Magere Brug, the **Koninklijk Thater Carré** keeps watch over the Amstel, while a parade of circus performers carved into is facade look as if they were carved

THE ARTS ⟨ THE LOWDOWN

from vanilla frosting. During the 19th century, the Carré Circus used to bring its wagon train of animals and performers to this spot every year, an event much anticipated by the locals. Oscar Carré schmoozed city officials and was eventually permitted to build a wooden circus hall as a permanent site. After fire ravaged a nearby neighborhood, city administrators decreed the structure to be a fire hazard and the whimsical, overwrought Theater Carré took its place. The circus tradition continues, however: elephants and the usual menagerie still perform in the indoor ring during the Christmas season. At other times of the year concerts, musicals, and recitals are held in the same space.

What's opera, doc?... After several moribund years of Italian tearjerkers and the like, opera attendance began climbing regularly around 1991; and the press gushed over performances. Opera's cachet grew, and a broader range of listeners started to pay attention (not just "Masterpiece Theatre" types). Most arts insiders credit Pierre Audi, the bold, well-respected artistic director of the Stopera's **Nederlandse Opera** (tel 020/625–5455), for the revival of interest. Audi left a stellar tenure at London's Almeida Theater in 1988 and took on the daunting task of creating an opera audience in a city that had previously responded only lukewarmly to this musical form, at least in traditional presentations. Audi has capitalized on the Dutch hunger for the new, not bothering to bid for world class tenors or to stage elaborate productions of the classics. Instead, he has staged minimalist performances by composers considered a shade offbeat, like Monteverdi and Debussy, as well as works by unknowns. If ticket sales alone are any indication, audiences have responded enthusiastically. Audi has also collaborated with artists in other media: Peter Greenaway teamed with composer Louis Andriessen to write a libretto, and Audi paired with conductor Harmut Haenchen to produce a new work. And in a 1995 production that some lemon-suckers called gimmicky (though the shows sold out consistently, so HA!), he collaborated with the ASKO Ensemble to stage an opera with live contemporary music in a film studio accessible only by boat. How's that for a night on the town? Opera tickets in Amsterdam run less than Dfl 90.

Classical sounds... There's nothing to write home about until you hear the music at the acoustically superior **Concertgebouw**, which celebrated its centennial in 1988. Home of the **Koninklijk Concertgebouworkest** (tel 020/ 671–8345), it's the bastion of orchestral, chamber, and choral music in Amsterdam, and it is stiffly correct looking, a proper and unremarkable hall. Strangely, the architect A. Van Gendt did not know music. He crowned the ornate facade with a pediment of Greco-Roman musicians and an oversized lute—and that's about as far as his interest in music went. Miraculously, inside, the acoustics are so good even Jessye Norman and Yo-Yo Ma go out of their way to praise it. Despite minor renovations over the years, the foundation threatened to collapse in 1983. Teams of engineers replaced rotting wooden pilings resting on sand with concrete piles driven 60 feet into the damp ground. A glass entrance added in 1988 was originally received about as well I.M. Pei's addition to the Louvre, but the hubbub has since died. From September through March this venerable venue is booked daily, often with performances in both the *Grote Zaal* (Great Hall) and the *Kleine Zaal* (Little Hall). The Grote Zaal, the preferred space, is reserved for big-ticket events. For many years the resident Concertebouworkest (known beyond the Netherlands border as the Royal Concertgebouw Orchestra) seemed bent on matching the building's stodgy atmosphere, turning in lackluster performances of tepid and predictable programs. Under the baton of Ricardo Chailly, the orchestra is attempting to loosen its 100-year-old image, enrich its repertoire, and expand its subscriber list. Instead of the safe menu of Brahms and Mahler preferred by former conductor Bernard Haitink, Chailly has injected Hindemith and Verese into the mix. He's also nudged a few older players into early retirement and replaced them with rising stars, aiming for a more robust-sounding ensemble.

Long coasting on a solid reputation for excellence, the **Amsterdam Baroque Orchestra & Choir** (tel 021/ 593–6050) tours widely, records frequently, and draws sell-out crowds when it performs in town. A founding father of the local orchestral music scene, Ton Koopman's artistic direction of the ABO&C draws from a plethora of baroque classics, including works by the oft-overlooked Dutch composer Peiter Hellendaal. Classical musicmeis-

THE ARTS ⟨ THE LOWDOWN

ters all agree that the Dutch excel at ensemble performance; and one example of stellar team work worth checking out is the **Nederlands Kamerkoor** (tel 020/662–5199), a group that blends three dozen voices like butter. Though the choir tours frequently, they do appear around the city in outdoor and indoor venues. Performances by the beleaguered **Nederlands Philharmonisch Orkest** (tel 020/627–0466) aren't as consistently excellent—or even as noteworthy. Perhaps it's fatigue. The NPO is trying to do the work of three orchestras. Formerly three ensembles (the Amsterdam Philharmonic, the Netherlands Chamber Orchestra, and the Netherlands Opera Orchestra), the NPO is now one orchestra forced to move back and forth between operatic, chamber, and symphonic repertoires. Government cutbacks have also strained their artistic resources. Much more interesting than the group is their memorable art nouveau home, the **Beurs van Berlage**.

Hash, bondage, and torture (stage left)... Most big-name art museums in major cities—and Amsterdam has plenty of these—have evening hours at least one night a week. On this front, the Dutch seem positively uncivilized. The big players (Rijksmuseum, Van Gogh Museum, and Stedelijk) all close with the work day. The only options for nighttime museumgoing are a handful of semi-cheesy though amusing sites that are like Amsterdam's answer to "Believe It or Not." These places claim a higher rung on the food chain by using the word "museum" in their names. The **Hash, Marijuana, and Hemp Museum** is the best of the admittedly motley half dozen. This homage to pot is sort of an oversized science project dedicated to the history, growth, and applications of the weed. A 15-minute video surveys herbal history. Pot paraphernalia is displayed behind glass counters, and books, magazines, hemp products, and seeds are for sale. And those two blank showcases in the museum? That's where cops confiscated some displays when they busted the museum several years back. Two Red Light District museums traffic in carnal knowledge: the **Sex Museum** and the **Erotic Museum**. Though the live, 3-D carnival and sleazy parade of the district itself outdoes the juvenile and poorly-shot porn of the **Sex Museum**, the five floors of drawings and exhibitions in the **Erotic Museum** make for a decidedly entertaining romp. (Somewhat surprisingly for one of the gay capitals of Europe, the focus here is resoundingly heterosexual.) With a push of a button, a flock of vibrators does a hula dance, a display that induces disturbing flashbacks of the June Taylor dancers writhing on the floor during the "Jackie Gleason Show." An S/M room provides an intro to the frontier between pain and pleasure. Other delightful diversions include hard-core porn videos; a phone-sex exhibit; fetish-wear; lingerie; an art collection with photos from Madonna's song of self, *Sex*; and sweet ink doodlings by John Lennon. One neighborhood over, on the Damrack from the Inquisition chair to the guillotine, the ensemble of medieval punishment and torture tools at the macabre **Torture Museum** is designed to thrill adolescents of all ages. Narrow passageways tunnel through an old three-story house. Lights flicker, throwing eerie shadows on an assortment of cruel devices from all parts of Europe. Plaques clearly articulate the history and the horrors of the acoutrements. In the Red Light District, skin is the canvas (in a friendlier way) at the **Tattoo Museum**, an intimate A-to-Z of tattooing. Fat albums bulge with images of tattoos and artists at work. A library stocks tattoo art and tomes on tattoo history. Attend one of the live demonstrations/ Q&A sessions if you're flirting with the idea of getting tattooed, branded, or pierced.

Men in tights, women in tutus... Two renown ballet companies reign at the forefront of the city's classical dance scene: Netherlands Nationale Ballet (tel 020/625–5455), housed in the **Muziektheater**; and Nederlands Dans Theater (NDT), based in The Hague. The Nationale Ballet has the numbers: it is the country's largest company and performs a repertoire of Balanchine ballets that rivals New York's, but balletgoers rue the company's lack of moxie and imagination. Some say things went limp in 1986 when the company moved into the 1,600-seat **Muziektheater** and needed to attract larger audiences to survive. If you want sass and style, try the NDT (tel 070/ 360–9931), which performs in various Amsterdam venues. Spearheading this daring company is artistic director Jiri Kylián, an influential Czech choreographer. The NDT always performs to live music and is more likely than the Nationale Ballet to experiment with works by younger choreographers like Lionel Hoche or Paul Lightfoot. Two offshoots of the NDT group dancers by age: NDT2 is a company of younger performers who dance the works of classical choreographers like Hans van Menen. NDT3 is a troupe of former NDT principals, all now 40 years plus, who perform experimental pieces.

The modern dance... Dutch tolerance has influenced the country's dance culture. A willingness to go out on limbs and to make calculated experimentation have helped secure the reputation Dutch (and Belgian) dancers have for innovative, professional work. Aided by the booming immigrant populations and the number of international artists residing in Amsterdam, modern dance here continues to expand, globalize, and gain international respect. Choreography comes first (before costuming, lighting, sets, and music); but the current rage here is incorporating other media and art forms, and to use unusual performance venues. Take Shusaku Takeuchi, a Japanese choreographer who has worked extensively in Holland for more than two decades, for example. He stages pyrotechnic works to live music in outdoor, waterfront sites. Other choreographers of note are Truus Bronkhorst, known locally as the First Lady of Dutch dance, and one known as the Twyla Tharp of Amsterdam, Beppie Blankert (his company is **Stichting Dansers Studio Beppie Blankert**). Many groups rove between different venues in town. The Hungarian minimalist Krisztina de Châtel heads a 20-year-old company, the **Dansgroup Kirsztina de Châtel** (tel 020/627–3970), and performs at the **Bellevue Theater**. Often premiering work in Amsterdam, the Arnhem-based **Introdans** (tel 020/623–5104) fuses modern, flamenco, ballet, and folk dances from around the world. **Danskern** (tel 020/623–5014) is known for cutting-edge performances, insider political humor, and a wider range of body types than are generally seen on dance stages, while the popular **Dansproduktie** (tel 020/623–5014) features outlandish, outré choreography that some have labeled "guerilla gymnastic." Of the many schools, two stand out as the cream of the crop, **Dans Werkplaats Amsterdam**, just west of Vondelpark, and **Liefde**, between Jordaan and the Museum District. Both hold open studio sessions and informal performances.

Het Veemtheater is just the kind of place where you'd expect to see a naked mime in white face, making strange hand gestures. Real estate agents would call the Shipping Quarter neighborhood "transitional." Artists have staked out this secluded industrial enclave near the port. Originally a warehouse, the theater retains a boxy, working-class feel. Just off Leidseplein, **Bellevue** is a trio of state-subsidized theaters where mime, Dutch-language theater, and modern dance troupes perform in intimate halls with a couple of hundred seats each; Krisztina de Châtel's troupe performs here regularly. **Felix Meritis**, a regal 18th-century building on Keizersgracht, was the nucleus of fringe theater in the 1970s. One of the city's oldest performance venues, the building today houses the Amsterdam Summer University and its **Shaffy Theater**, which showcases small-scale theater, video presentations, and seminars. Modern dance and ballet perfomances by such highbrow troupes as the **Nederlands Dans Theater (NDT)** are staged here. No more than five dozen chairs can squeeze into **Captain Fiddle**, a cozy weekend performance space for dancers near the Red Light District.

Dance folk... Folk dance in Amsterdam is far less popular than modern, but it has begun to gain wider audiences in recent years as the world continues to culturally cross-pollinate. The city's only strong folk troupe, **Folkloristisch Danstheater**, rarely performs Dutch works. Instead, resident guest choreographers work with the troupe of two dozen dancers to stage religious and ceremonial dances from points beyond, particularly Eastern Europe.

A little English on the stage... Most of the English-language theater productions in Amsterdam are staged by visiting companies and touring groups—everything from *Les Mis* to whatever Neil Simon opus has been exhumed for revival. Even though the city is aswim in English and undoubtedly has the English-language theatergoing audience to support a wider selection, Amsterdam has only one bona fide English-language theater company with its own space—the **Stalhouderij** (which means "the stable"). Housed in a former livery, the miniscule performance space is the scene for competent contemporary and classic productions. At **Badhuis Theater de Bochel**, a former bathhouse, all the productions are in English, though the theater has no company in residence. Eastern European works are the current rage here. Other English-only theater companies include Yell Theatre, Amsterdam Chamber Theatre (ACT), European-American Theatre, and Panache. Panache, the most active of the lot, stages about three productions a season at various venues around the city, one of the most charming of which is the 17th-century **Kleine Komedie**. Fronting the Amstel and near to the Muziektheater, the plush interior seats 500 and is one of the most popular halls for European touring cabaret and stand-up comedy. Smaller venues that do English include **De Balie** off Leidseplein—where you're more likely to find politically oriented debates and lectures, though the occasional contemporary theater performance is offered—and **Bovenzaal**, a small space inside the baroque and fanciful Stadsschouwburg.

The (Dutch) theatah... Unless your grasp of Dutch is at least very good, sitting in an audience watching a play performed in Dutch will most likely be a giant snooze. If Dutch is music to your mouth, some of the Dutch masters of the 18th and 19th centuries who penned what are today called classics are Hooft, Vondel, and Brodero. Though productions of Dutch standbys are less common on Amsterdam stages today, works by these three playwrights usually show up at some theater every season; they're often given a modern twist that renders them palatable for today's thrill-hungry audiences. Some of the American and British theater's most well-known playwrights, both classic and contemporary, have had their works translated into Dutch—Pinter, Miller, Stoppard—and even if you know each scene by heart, you will be lost without a working knowledge of Dutch. That being said, for the more adventurous and perhaps sociologically oriented, a night of experimental theater in Dutch will be well worth the guilders and the recurring moments of confusion. If you manage to stay awake during the two-hour melange of movement, dance, and spoken word, you may find that the symbolism transcends language—so why not try it? It may border on the ridiculous. But Amsterdam's unflagging reputation as a European center for provocative experimental theater—and attendant ardently arty crowds—might be incentive enough. And here's more: it's cheap. Tickets usually don't run more than Dfl 20 or so. One of the city's oldest streets, Nes, is the center for experimental, radical, and contemporary theater. Think Off-Off Broadway meets Cirque du Soleil with a bit of Laurie Anderson thrown in. The fringe works are most often staged in small theaters like **De Brakke Grond**, **Cosmic Theater**, **Frascati**, and **De Engelenbak**, where banners announcing each theater flutter outside gabled canalhouses.

In addition to the cluster on Nes, theaters such as **Polanen Theatre** and **Theater Instituut Nederland** host new works every June as part of the International Theater School Festival, a two-week showcase of experimental productions. Most are in Dutch, but English works show up frequently on the schedule. Venues where you are more likely to find a production staged in English are **University Theatre**, a more mainstream contemporary theater that is home to the Caterwauling Company, and **Villa Baranka**, a theater-*cum*-salon that holds about 40 people during weekend performances of music and theater.

Improv... Originating in Chicago (who'd have guessed?), **Boom Chicago Theater**'s improv comedy troupe gives humorous takes on American politics and cross-cultural faux pas for mostly tourist audiences. In the early 1990s three members of the troupe imported the stateside approach to comedy in a dinner-theater setting. Circular tables of patrons eat roast beef and drink vats of white wine while the group does send-ups of Bill Clinton, delves into local happenings, and makes fun of those wacky Americans.

Al fresco theater... Though Amsterdam weather is lousy, with only infrequent days of sunshine, that meteorological disappointment is offset by summer's extended daylight. During summer, the sun doesn't set until 10pm and dusk lingers for close to an hour, caping the city in the golden magic of twilight. During these daylit nighttime hours, the Dutch spend every possible moment outdoors, and city theater companies take their shows, often performed in English, to **Openluchttheater Vondelpark**, **Openluchttheater Amsterdamse Bos**, or **Amstelpark**. Vondelpark's theater hosts outdoor music concerts as well as theater productions of classics by Shakespeare, Chekhov, and Pinter (sometimes in English, sometimes in

Dutch). The 1,800-seat amphitheater in Amsterdamse Bos has a regal entryway through the wooded park. Greco-Roman statues line a pathway to the performance space, where, appropriately enough, traditional theatrical works are performed on summer's evenings. *De Parade* is a summer-only set of tents erected at Amstelpark where circus acts, musicians, and thespians perform.

The movies... No film buff would ever claim that the Dutch embrace celluloid the way the French do. Amsterdammers are not the world's most avid filmgoers—there are fewer than five dozen cinema screens across Amsterdam. Not a lot of choices, but you will find a lot of variety when it comes to ambience and decor; the city's movie houses range from the gonzo, low-budget **Exploding Cinema**, which shows grainy art films projected against a pockmarked wall, to the magnificent art deco **Tuschinski** cinema, a gala throwback to the extravagances of the gilded Hollywood era. Non-Dutch films are always subtitled. So don't fret; you won't have to witness Julia Roberts emote in an unfamiliar guttural tongue. Conversely, keep in mind that if you come across that Wertmüller or Almodovar film you've been dying to see, you may very well still be left out in the linguistic cold, since these films are also shown in the original tongue and subtitled in Dutch. For Hollywood first-runs (which often show up here just weeks after they've debuted in the States), head for the area around Leidseplein and Rembrandtplein. Favorite spots include the **Alfa**, where you'll find intelligent English-language films that usually steers clear of blockbusters. The **Alhambra** is a small theater that specializes in showing films you thought weren't playing anywhere anymore. The **Calypso and Bellevue Cinerama** are neighboring film houses that specialize in first-run European and American films, while **Cinecenter**, a small house, splits its fare between French and English films. And **Riksbioscoop**, the Dutch version of Dollar Theater, shows last year's top films for a *rijksdaalder* (a Dfl 2.50 coin). As in the States, Friday and Saturday nights are the busiest at the box office; these are also the nights when the price of a ticket rises by as much as five guilders. It's prudent to buy tickets to evening weekend shows earlier in the day or week. Tickets can be reserved over the telephone—for a service charge of a guilder or two—by calling cinemas directly, though you can't use a credit card to pay. *De Week Agenda*, a weekly brochure available at clubs, restaurants, and movie theaters, lists current runs. Other sources of information are *Uitkrant*, the Wednesday edition of *Het Parool*, and *Amsterdams Stadsblad*. The free monthly magazine *De Filmkrant* is in Dutch, but it's easy enough to decipher the listings even if you are not fluent. Films change every Thursday. There are usually a few screenings in the afternoon and evening, and midnight shows are becoming increasingly popular. Instead of refreshment counters that sell Junior Mints, Goobers, and jumbo vats of popcorn, in Amsterdam's movie theaters you'll find cafes that sell coffee and sandwiches in addition to ice cream, sweets, and assorted junk food. The cafe at **The Movies** on Haarlemmenstraat near Jordaan also has a swell jukebox with sixties tunes and presents live jazz or folk bands on weekends; this place is definitely worth a visit if only to ogle the painstakingly restored thirties interior. Some cinemas have bars or restaurants. The bars at **Tuschinksi**, **Filmmuseum**, **Rialto**, and **Kriterion** are particularly lively spots, especially on weekends. Surprisingly, cigarette smoking is verboten inside all movie theaters (screening rooms may be the *only* places in Amsterdam where you'll find a smoke-free environment). In the middle of the film—usually in a pivotal scene—comes the *pauze*, a 15-minute intermission. Recently some mainstream theaters have picked up on the public's disdain for the break and advertise which films are being shown *geen pauze* ("without an interval").

Film festivals... The city's biggest filmfest is the seven-day **Nederlands Filmdagen**, a sort of Dutch Sundance Festival held the third week of September. Hundreds of new Dutch films—from shorts to features—and TV shows are premiered. Student work is screened. Awards are bestowed. Galas are staged. Local talent gone big time is fêted. In December, Amsterdam hosts the annual **International Documentary Film Festival**. Many of the earnest documentarians showing their latest projects and competing for awards are graduates of the internationally respected Nederlandse Film en Televisie Academie (NFTA), an offshoot of the city's prestigious art school, Amsterdam Hogeschool Voor de Kunsten. Entry to the

NFTA is highly competitive; only 200 students annually gain admission to the rigorous, four-year curriculum. Alums include Jan de Bont, whose resume includes the recent blockbuster *Twister* as well as *Speed*, *The Jewel of the Nile*, and *Ruthless People*; and Paul Verhoeven, who has directed *Robocop*, *Total Recall*, and *Basic Instinct*. Many Dutch filmgoers lament that Dutch actors and filmmakers are better known abroad than in the Netherlands. American audiences are probably most familiar with actors Rutger Hauer of *Blade Runner* and Jerome Krabbé, who starred in *The Prince of Tides*.

Art films... The ticket prices are cheaper, the surroundings tend to be less glitzy, the snack bars don't have as many treats, and the patrons are less mainstream than the ones waiting in line to see *Independence Day*. Instead of first-runs and blockbuster hits, *filmhuizen* specialize in offbeat films (like *The Attack of the Killer Tomatoes*), retrospectives, documentaries (*The Bhopal Tragedy*), and film festivals. The **Studio Theater**, hidden behind the Stadsschouwburg, shows obscure gems, as does the **Rialto**. On Sundays the **Desmet**, a classically designed art deco theater with turrets, chandeliers, and ornate detailing, screens gay and lesbian films. Just a short stroll from Centraal Station is **De Boomspijker**, known for international documentaries popular with an appropriately artsy crowd. The **Netherlands Filmmuseum** in Vondelpark offers retrospectives (Laurel and Hardy, Buñuel), cult films (*Duel*, Spielberg's first), and summer outdoor screenings on an upstairs terrace overlooking ponds and the jogging paths weaving through the park. **Kriterion** offers an international mix on its two screens; they tend to be heavy on French erotica and thrillers of any nation. The 1913 **Bioscope de Uitkijk**, the city's oldest cinema, screens classics without a *pauze* in its intimate 158-seat theater; unfortunately, because of the management's "no refreshments" policy, you'll have to smuggle in your own munchies.

Hit it, Pearl... Church organ concerts are offered year round in Amsterdam. Though there are 42 church organs in the city, the most spectacular are the Great Organs of **Nieuwe Kerk** and **Oude Kerk**. The Nieuwe Kerk organ was designed by Jacob van Campen; its gilded casing anointed with cherubs and angels blinds with its sheen. Magnificent and imposing, it sits behind an ornately carved pulpit that took 15 years for artisans to complete. The organ recitals here emphasize classic works by Bach, Handel, and the other usual suspects from Music Appreciation 101. The city's other Great Organ is housed in Oude Kerk, a refuge in the sleaze of the Red Light District. Oak cloaks the instrument, which is outfitted with 54 gilded pipes and eight bellows and a holy coterie of carved wooden saints. **Westerkerk** has two claims to fame among Amsterdam's houses of worship: it has the city's tallest tower and Rembrandt is buried here. On Tuesdays, **carillon** bell concerts resound from its steeple, and throughout the year the church hosts chamber music, choral concerts, and organ recitals. The concerts at the 17th-century **Engelse Kerk** run the gamut from modern to baroque, from choirs to soloists. The interior is less spectacular than that of its brethren "kerks," but the setting is one of the city's most picturesque—it's tucked into Amsterdam's most beautiful *hofje* (hidden courtyard). **Waalse Kerk** and **Amstelkerk** host choral ensembles, chamber music, and solo musicians for evening concerts. Even musicians who could draw larger crowds than the venue can accommodate choose to perform here because of the rich acoustics provided by the soaring ceilings.

Rock and jazz... Amsterdammers are rock music zealots and when one of the big names—like Tina Turner, the Rolling Stones, or Hootie & the Blowfish—comes to town they pack the stadium or concert hall. The futuristic, metallic **Amsterdam Arena** on the south side of town, with 150,000 seats and potent klieg lights, is the newest and roomiest space. If you're near the southern 'burbs, check out the **RAI** Center, frequently used to host trade expos, boat shows, and conferences, but often its 1,750-seat capacity accomodates rock concerts. The most intimate and aesthetically pleasing performance spaces for visiting rock and jazz musicians are three clubs in the city center, all respected elders in Amsterdam's music scene: **Paradiso**, a former church, and **Melkweg**, a former dairy, have popular dance clubs and regularly host local rock bands and U.S. and Euro-touring acts like Phish, Joan Osborne, and Spacehog. **Bimhuis**, or "Bim," as the locals call it, is a large, popular jazz club and performance hall.

THE ARTS ⟲ THE LOWDOWN

It actually lost some cozy ambience recently when it enlarged its performance space (it's now the size of a small auditorium) and added a sleek, modern bar.

Alt.performance, squats, and beyond... Fringe, avant-garde, and experimental theater has always found fertile ground in Amsterdam. Since the 1980s, when the government began making hefty cuts in arts programs, the tenacity of counterculture theater has been tried, but it continues to flourish with smaller budgets, shorter company lifespans, and performance spaces in squats and somewhat rougher venues (where overhead costs aren't a concern). Avant-garde theater is a fickle creature in general: companies and venues aren't known for longevity or consistency. Today's innovative fringe groups have names like Art & Pro, Nieuw West, and Orkater. They'll likely be gone tomorrow, so catch while catch can. The most mainstream—and the cushiest—of the alternative venues is **Soeterijn**, the small theater appended to the Tropeninstituut, an organization that promotes and studies peoples and cultures from warm-weather climates. Balinese dancers, Tibetan choral monks, and folk musicians are on the bill here. At **Westergasfabriek**, a former gas factory now converted and subdivided into performance spaces, multimedia art happenings are the thing. Recently the Triple-X International Arts Festival, an eclectic group of international and performance artists offered pieces with names like "CyberChrist," "Pain," and "Wash Nonsense." The **Transformatorhuis Toneelgroep Amsterdam** (tel 020/621–1211) is the performance group in residence. At three squat spaces, **Vrieshuis Amerika** near Centraal Station, **Onafhankelijk Cultureel Centrum In It** near Vondelpark, and **Itonia** near the Red Light District, the scene is neo-beat and peopled with backpackers, underground artistes, and raver Gen Xers with open disdain for the bourgeoisie and anyone older than 40. Performances at all three tend to be disorganized (and a bit infantile). You're most likely to hear bad poetry accompanied by bongo beats or witness a collection of free-form sculpture spiked with stalagtites entitled *Angst.* Still, the gonzo, anything-goes, and power-to-the-people philosophy in these squatted spaces and underground venues is something you're unlikely to find anywhere else.

THE ARTS ◟ THE LOWDOWN

Monuments and memorials... Dozens of monuments, memorials, and historic markers scattered across the city are often overlooked by travelers who discount the artistic merit and insight of these public works. They are all well lit, except the **Homomonument**, which is nevertheless a compelling sight at night, illuminated by memorial candles. Progressive and unusual, it's the only public work in the world that commemorates the persecution of gays and lesbians. Sculptor Karin Daan's understated trio of pink granite triangles forms a slab installed at the water level of Keizersgracht. Flowers and candles are testimony to private struggles. On World Aids Day, December 1, the monument is a rallying point for the homosexual community. World War II and the role the Dutch played in resisting the Nazis and forming an underground to shelter Jews are the most popular subjects of city monuments. The most modern, **Jewish Resistance Monument**, pays respect to the Holocaust and those who perished during the resistance. The stark black column is inscribed with the words, "If my eyes were a well of tears, I would cry day and night for the fallen fighters of my beloved people." The **Ravensbrückmonument** is a Holocaust memorial dedicated to the women "who defied fascism to the end." An illuminated silver column throws shadows on panels inscribed with names and text about the atrocities. In February 1941 city dock and transit workers went on strike to protest the cruelty perpetrated on the Jews by the Nazis—in particular, the first German roundup and execution of 400 Dutch Jews. The **Dokwerker Monument** on JD Meijerplein across from Waterlooplein (and in the heart of *Jodenhoek*, the traditionally Jewish neighborhood) strikes a resonant chord: a lone, plaintive figure gazes forlornly toward the sky. Each February 25, a commemorative ceremony is held here. The memorial that dominates the center of Dam Square is the **Nationaal Monument**, a 70-foot-high obelisk that pays homage to the Dutch who died during World War II. Oversized lions guard the base, behind which are sealed urns containing dirt from each of the Dutch provinces and colonies, including Suriname, the Dutch Antilles, and Indonesia.

THE LOWDOWN ◯ THE ARTS

The Index

Alhambra. An unremarkable and uncrowded film house with four theaters that show box-office biggies about six months after they've burst onto the pop-culture scene.... *Tel 020/ 623–3192. Weteringschans 134; tram 4, 6, 7, or 10.*

Alfa. This former dance hall is now an MGM art-film house that specializes in English-language films and the occasional premiere.... *Tel 020/627–8806. Hirschgebouw, Leidseplein; tram 1, 2, 5, 6, 7, 10, or 11.*

Amstelpark. A verdant patch in the southwestern burb of Buitenveldert visually anchored by the Rieker windmill that stands on the southern tip of the park. In summer months, evening open-air theater and musical concerts are performed gratis.... *No telephone. Europaboulevard; tram 4, bus 69 or 169.*

Amstelkerk. Designed as a temporary structure in the late 1600s, this wooden church overlooking the Reguliersgracht and Prinsengracht canals is a pristine venue for chamber music concerts, classical music recitals, and choral ensembles.... *Tel 020/622–0774; Amstelveld 2, tram 4.*

Amstelveen Cultural Centrum. An artless, mid-sized exhibition space and cultural center on the outskirts of the city center.... *Tel 020/645–8444. Plein 1960, Amstelveen; bus 64 or 66.*

Amsterdam Arena. This futuristically designed 150,000-seat sports and concert stadium in the southwestern suburbs opened in August 1996. Home of Ajax, the city's Cup-winning soccer team, and venue for big-name visiting acts like Tina Turner, who inaugurated it.... *Tel 020/691–2906. Zuidoost, Metro Strandvliet.*

Artis Planetarium. Part of a sprawling zoological complex showcasing flora, fauna, and animals. The planetarium's evening shows contain the usual starfest and parade of planets that glitter to contemporary music. Shows are narrated in Dutch and later encapsulated (sort of a Cliff's Notes approach) in four languages, including English.... *Tel 020/ 523–3452. Plantage Kerklaan; tram 7, 9, or 14.*

Bachzaal. A small concert hall that is part of the Sweelinck Conservatorium in the Museum District. Students at the conservatorium hold irregularly scheduled concerts—chamber, classical, and the like—that are often free.... *Tel 020/ 664–7641. Bachstraat 7; tram 5 or 24.*

Badhuis Theater de Bochel. Productions at this former bathhouse are frequently in English.... *Tel 020/668–5102. Andreas Bonnstraat 28; tram 3, 6, 7, or 10; Metro Weesperplein.*

De Balie. A politically tinged center of international culture that hosts lectures, seminars, debates, theater, music, and dance. Mostly in Dutch, though occasional programs are hosted in English.... *Tel 020/623–2904. Kleine Gartmansplansoen 1; tram 1, 2, 5, 6, 7, 10, or 11.*

Bellevue. Traditional dramas (in Dutch) is the primary offering in this state–subsidized trio of theaters just off Leidseplein, though no–Dutch–needed cabaret acts, dance companies, and mime troupes stage experimental works here as well.... *Tel 020/624–7248. Leidsekade 90; tram 1, 2, 5, 6, 7, 10, or 11.*

Beurs van Berlage. A stunning homage to Dutch art nouveau, this former stock exchange is today the official home of the Nederlands Philharmonisch Orkest and the Nederlands Kamerorkest. Don't miss the interior frieze that charts the economic evolution of man—Adam morphs into a stockbroker.... *Tel 020/627–0466. Damrak 243; tram 4, 9, 16, 24, or 25.*

Bimhuis. The revered elder of Amsterdam's jazz club, though some say it's lost a bit of its soul over the past years as Bim's become a shade more glamorous and modernized. The big jazz names perform here.... *Tel 020/623–1361. Oude Schans 73–77, tram 9 or 14.*

THE ARTS ⟨ THE INDEX

Bioscope de Uitkijk. The city's oldest movie theater screens classics without the deadening *pauze*. No snack bar, though, so you'll have to try to hide your Gouda *broodje* in your pocket.... *Tel 020/623–7460. Prinsengracht 452; tram 1, 2, 5, or 11.*

Boom Chicago Theater. Hackneyed, safe American improv dinner theater with material as original as what you'd find on a cruise ship. The kind of thing you'd take your grandparents to.... *Tel 020/625–5454. Lijnbaansgracht 238; tram 1, 2, 5, 6, 7, 10, or 11.*

De Boomspijker. A small film house that screens lots of special-interest and/or artsy documentaries; just a short trek away from Centraal Station.... *Tel 020/626–4002. Rechtboomssloot 52; bus 22, 32, 33, 34, 35, 36, or 39; Metro Nieuwmarkt.*

Bovenzaal. See **Stadsssschouwburg.**

De Brakke Grond. This Flemish cultural center hosts the oh-so-occasional performance in English. Art exhibitons break the language barrier and the place throws a mean cocktail party when a show opens.... *Tel 020/626–6866. Nes 45; tram 4, 9, 14, 16, 24, or 25.*

Calypso and Bellevue Cinerama. American mall-style, side-by-side cinema houses with a common box office. Both host first-run U.S. and European flicks.... *Tel 020/623–4876. Marnixstraat 400; tram 1, 2, 5, 7, 10, or 11.*

Captain Fiddle. A typical representative of the dozens of small venues around the city that sponsor modern dance productions.... *Tel 020/626–0363. Kloveniersburgwal 86; tram 4, 14, 16, 24, or 25; Metro Nieuwmarkt.*

Carillons. Five carillons in the city—Oudekerk, Zuiderkerk, Westerkerk, Koninklijk Royal Paleis, and Munttoren—echo their bell music every 15 minutes, much as they have since 1510 when they first began pealing. Occasional concerts are held at all carillons, but the music is less deafening and more poetic when heard echoing forlornly through the streets.

Cinecenter. The biggest drawback is the lack of air-conditioning at this quartet of movie screens across the street from the Melkweg. French, Spanish, and English-language films are the fare.... *Tel 020/623–6615. Lijnbaansgracht 236; tram 1, 2, 5, 6, 7, 10, or 11.*

Concertgebouw. Performers rave publicly about the acoustic perfection of this venerable venue with two halls—*Grote Zaal* (Large Hall), where the big names perform, and *Kleine Zaal* (Small Hall), host to chamber musicians and lower-rung soloists. The Concertgebouworkest resides here under the baton of Riccardo Chailly.... *Tel 020/671–8345. Concertgebouwplein 2–6; tram 3, 5, 12, or 16.*

Cosmic Theater. Main orbit (the name is a big, fat clue) for avant-garde and experimental art: dance, theater, improv. Occasional English-language works are performed, but it's worth seeing a play in Dutch just to get a load of their innovative approach to theater.... *Tel 020/622–8858. Nes 75; tram 4, 9, 14, 16, 24, or 25.*

Cristofori. Local piano manufacturer with showroom space on Prinsengracht that occasionally sponsors chamber and classical music concerts (like the annual August outdoor concert in front of the Pulitzer Hotel).... *Tel 020/626–8485. Prinsengracht 579; tram 13, 14, or 17.*

Dans Werkplaats Amsterdam. Premiere dance studio that hosts free, casual, modern dance performances.... *Tel 020/ 689–1789. Arie Biemondstraat 107; tram 1, 6, 7, 11, or 17.*

Desmet. Gay and lesbian films are screened in this splendid Art Deco cinema on Sundays; worldwide art films (with Dutch subtitles) are the main offering.... *Tel 020/627–3434. Plantage Middenlaan 4A; tram 7, 9, or 14.*

Dokwerker Monument. A plaintive figure gazes forlornly skyward in this monument commemorating dock and transit workers who went on strike in February 1941 to protest Nazis' mistreatment of the Jews.... *No telephone. Jonas Daniel Meijerplein; tram 4, 9, or 14; Metro Waterlooplein.*

Ebony Band. A fledgling band of wind, percussion, brass, and string players from the Rotterdam and Concertgebouw orchestras dedicated to playing forbidden little known music (i.e. pieces banned by the Nazis, obscure composers, music from the Spanish Civil War).... *Tel 020/664–0175.*

THE INDEX

THE ARTS

De Engelenbak. One of the theaters along Nes, the narrow street that has become Amsterdam's version of Off-Off Broadway.... *Tel 020/624–0394. Nes 64; tram 4, 9, 14, 16, 24, or 25.*

De Engelse Kerk. A charming 15th-century church with a medieval tower on the southern end of the Begijnhof. Classical and chamber music concerts are held here in summer.... *Tel 020/624–9665. Begijnhof 48; tram 1, 2, 5, or 11.*

Erotic Museum. Bring the K-Y Jelly. Stimulating collection of porno/erotica, including drawings by John Lennon, German bestiality cartoons, and excerpts from Madonna's *Sex* book.... *Tel 020/624–7303. Oudezijds Achterburgwal 54; tram 4, 9, 16, 24, or 25. Open daily until 1am.*

Exploding Cinema. This angst-heavy indie film house in a squat, six-story building along Het IJ shows earnest films that look like the senior projects of art school students.... *Tel 065/463–3700. Vrieshuis Amerika, Oostelijke Handelskade 25; bus 28, 32, or 39.*

Felix Meritis. A neo-classical theater, circa–late 1700s, is today the home of the Amsterdam Summer University theater and dance performances. The experimental theater group *Maatschappij Discordia* calls this home and often lets the public in for a free look at work in progress.... *Tel 020/623–1311. Keizersgracht 324; tram 1, 2, 5, or 11.*

Filmmuseum Cinematheek. See **Netherlands Filmmuseum.**

Folkoristisch Danstheater. This corps of two dozen dancers performs original international folk dances commissioned by guest choreographers.... *Tel 020/623–5359. Kloveniersburgwal 87; tram 9 or 14; Metro Nieuwmarkt.*

Frascati. Small theater specializing in Dutch experimental works. The adjacent trendy cafe of the same name is a good place to sneak off to, if the somber Dutch thespians just aren't reaching you.... *Tel 020/623–5723. Nes 63; tram 4, 9, 14, 16, 24, or 25.*

THE INDEX

THE ARTS

The Hash, Marijuana, and Hemp Museum. *Reefer Madness* gets museumfied. Included in this exhibit that showcases the herb, its history, its uses, and its attendant paraphernalia, are a grow room, a small library, video presentations, and a fascinating catalog of medicinal uses.... *Tel 020/623–5961. Oudezijds Achterburgwal 148; tram 4, 9, 16, 24, or 25. Open daily until 10pm.*

Het Veemtheater. A warehouse saved from neglect and converted into an out-of-the-way venue for movement theater including mime, modern dance, and contortion.... *Tel 020/626–0112. Van Diemenstraat 410; tram 3 to terminus, then bus 35.*

Homomonument. It's not surprising that a city that is so tolerant and well-educated about homosexuality should be the site of the world's first memorial to persecuted gays and lesbians. These three triangles of pink marble jutting into Keizersgracht might otherwise go unnoticed were it not for all the flowers and candles pilgrims leave behind.... *Westermarkt; tram 13, 14, or 17.*

De IJsbreker Musiekcentrum. This contemporary music center is well-established on the international scene and offers a melange of local and global experimenters. The adjoining cafe is one of the city's best for people-watching and artsy-fartsy posturing.... *Tel 020/668–1805. Weesperzijde 23; tram 3; bus 51, 53, or 54.*

Itonia. A renegade Wednesday-only performance space in a squatted building. Poetry readings, plays, interpretive dance, experimental filmmaking—all in English.... *No telephone. Kloveniersburgwal 20; tram 4, 9, or 14. Closed Thur–Tue.*

Jewish Resistance Monument. This somber black column designed by the Glatt brothers commemorates the horrors of the Holocaust.... *No telephone. Zwanenburgwal at Amstel; tram 9 or 14; Metro Waterlooplein.*

Kleine Komedie. Established in 1786, this is one of the city's oldest theaters. Most productions are staged in Dutch, but occasionally, community playhouse-type English-language shows appear on the bill.... *Tel 020/624–0534. Amstel 56, tram 4.*

THE ARTS ⟨ THE INDEX

Koninklijk Theater Carré. The jesters, dancers, and clowns adorning the facade of the Carré are testimony to the circus that occupied this site on the Amstel in the 19th century. Today the circus is still performed at Christmas, but the rest of the year the venue hosts music concerts.... *Tel 020/622–5225. Amstel 115–125; tram 6, 7, or 10; Metro Weesperplein.*

Kriterion. Check out this volunteer-run movie theater at midnight on weekends, when it screens American cult films and French erotica. The downstairs bar is popular.... *Tel 020/623–1708. Roeterstraat 170; tram 6, 7, or 10, Metro Weesperplein.*

Liefde. A modern dance school that sponsors public performances of works in progress in its studio.... *Tel 020/683–3114. Da Costakade 102; tram 12, 13, or 14.*

Melkweg. Once a milk house, this club is now a leading light of the city's pop music scene. It has a bar, a coffeeshop that sells hash and pot, and enough space for visiting rock bands and their fans.... *Tel 020/624–8492. Lijnbaansgracht 234; tram 1, 2, 5, 6, 7, 10, or 11.*

The Movies. Renovated in the 1970s to recapture the grandeur of its 1928 predecessor, The Movies boasts a swell cafe (featuring live jazz and folk music and a kicking jukebox) and a bill of international, out-of-the-mainstream films à la Buñuel, Almodovar, Wertmüller, et al.... *Tel 020/638–6016. Haarlemmerdijk 161, tram 3.*

Muziektheater. The locals call it "Stopera," and the prevailing public sentiment about the modern, crescent-shaped building is that it is an architectural abomination. A choice Amstel riverfront location with 1,600 seats, it is the home of the Nationale Ballet and the Nederlands Opera.... *Tel 020/625–5455. Amstel 3; tram 9, or 14.*

Mystèr 2000. Multimedia cybercenter about covers it. Inside this former textile factory in Jordaan, you'll find an Internet-wired cafe, studios, performance spaces, dance floor, smart bar, and throngs of people who subscribe to *Wired* and slouch toward nihilism.... *Tel 020/620–2970. Lijnbaansgracht 92; tram 10.*

Nationaal Monument. The grandiose, 70-foot high obelisk in the Dam that commemorates those from the Netherlands who died during World War II. Oversized lions stand guard around sealed urns containing dirt from each of the Dutch provinces and colonies.... *No telephone. Dam; tram 4, 9, 14, 16, 24, or 25.*

Netherlands Filmmuseum. Cult films, summer outdoor screenings, documentaries—this government-subsidized museum housed in a former teahouse in Vondelpark is a primo film- *and* people-watching spot. Café Vertigo, the adjacent terrace cafe beckons for post-film beers (see The Bar and Cafe Scene).... *Tel 020/589–1400. Vondelpark 3; tram 1, 2, 3, 5, 6, 11, or 12.*

Nieuwe Kerk. This 14th-century church on Dam Square hosts art exhibitions, recitals on the gargantuan gilded organ designed by Jacob Van Campen, and evening concerts of Bach, Beethoven, et al.... *Tel 020/626–8168. Dam Square; tram 1, 2, 4, 5, 9, 13, 14, 17, 24, or 25.*

OCCII. At the far end of Vondelpark, this music hall has an informal, collegiate feel and a good reputation for launching local bands.... *Tel 020/671–7778. Amstelveenseweg 134; tram 2 or 6.*

Onafhankelijk Cultureel Centrum In It. Wear a beret. Sneer at the bourgeoisie. Soulfully inhale filterless cigarettes. Change your name to Why. There's no better place in Amsterdam to ponder existential angst than at this squat club/cabaret/performance space/dance hall/sauna/theater/It mecca, the cornerstone of Amsterdam's thriving experimental multimedia arts scene in underground venues.... *Tel 020/671–7778. Amstelveenseweg 134, tram 6.*

Openluchttheater Amsterdamse Bos. The city's largest park (2,000 acres) features an open-air theater where the works of Brecht, Chekov, Shakespeare, and other dramatists are performed for free on summer evenings.... *Tel 020/638–3847. Amstelveenseweg; bus 170, 171, or 172.*

Openluchttheater Vondelpark. In the summer, Amsterdam's version of Central Park hosts an eclectic series of music concerts (salsa, classical guitar, Mongolian Boys Choir) that provides beautiful and free noise…. *No telephone. Southwest of the city center; tram 1, 2, 3, 5, 6, 7, 10, 11, or 12.*

Oude Kerk. Organ music concerts reverberate through this majestic church—a 14th-century Gothic basilica—in the Red Light District. Or is that cherubim and seraphim just whistling Dixie…. *Tel 020/625–8284. Oudekerksplein 23; all trams, buses, and Metro to Centraal Station.*

Paradiso. Reincarnated from an abandoned church, this relentlessly popular rock club and dance hall is where visiting big-name acts like Joan Osborne and Del Amitri perform…. *Tel 020/626–4521. Weteringschans 6–8; tram 1, 2, 5, 7, 10, or 11.*

Polanen Theatre. You'll need more than tourist Dutch to understand the experimental theater staged at this tiny venue…. *Tel 020/682–1311. Polanenstraat 174, bus 22 or 35.*

Pulitzer Hotel. A group of canal homes that have been reborn as one of the city's most endearing hotels. In August each year, the hotel and Christofori's (the famous piano makers) sponsor a twilight concert of classical music performed from a barge moored on Prinsengracht…. *Tel 020/523–5235. Prinsengracht 315–331; tram 13, 14, or 17.*

RAI. This cavernous, bloodless exhibition hall in the southern 'burbs hosts the mega-events: rock shows, expos, boat shows…. *Tel 020/644–8651. Europaplein 12; tram 4; bus 15, 51, 60, 69, 158, or 159.*

Ravensbrückmonument. A Holocaust memorial, erected in 1975, dedicated to the women of Ravensbrück. An inscription on metal panels on the central column reads, "For women who defied fascism to the end"…. *No telephone. Museumplein; tram 2, 3, 5, 12, or 16.*

Rialto. This movie theater schedules an aesthetically-educated mix of artsy international flicks heavy on Italian pathos films, American gangster B&Ws, and satisfying French schmaltz…. *Tel 020/675–3994. Ceintuurbaan 338; tram 3, 12, 24, or 25.*

Riksbioscoop. The Dutch equivalent of the Dollar Theater where last year's American blockbuster films are only Dfl 2.50 a pop. Ah-nuld, Sly, Julia Roberts, and Tom Cruise rule here.... *Tel 020/624–3639. Reguliersbreestraat 31; tram 4, 9, 14, 16, 24, or 25.*

Sex Museum. If you've strolled through the Red Light District, or even just channel-surfed over the Playboy Channel, this museum will be ho-hum. The only reason to fork over the guilders for admission is to pose for a Kodak moment in the 7-foot-high penis chair.... *Tel 020/622–8376. Damrak 18, all trams and buses to Centraal Station, Metro Centraal Station.*

Shaffy Theater. See **Felix Meritis.**

Soeterijn. Performance space in the **Tropeninstituut**, an institute devoted to studying and promoting the works of the Tropics' indigenous peoples.... *Tel 020/568–8500. Maurits-kade 63, tram 9 or 14.*

Stadsschouwburg. The city's municipal theater, a balanced baroque building with 1,000 seats. Most productions are in Dutch, though current director Cox Habbema has laced the annual program with productions in English. A smaller space, called Bovenzaal, hosts less elaborate productions.... *Tel 020/624–2311. Leidseplein 26; tram 1, 2, 5, 6, 7, 10, or 11.*

Stalhouderij. Amsterdam's only English-language theater company has an enthusiastic coterie of patrons and needn't rely on government subsidy. Productions, ranging from Shakespeare to Albee, are staged every two months in the company's tiny space.... *Tel 020/626–2282. 1e Bloemwarsstraat 4; tram 13, 14, or 17.*

Stichting Dansers Studio Beppie Blankert. Respected local modern dance troupe with a fluid line-up of dancers and choreographers led by Beppie Blankert (the Twyla Tharp of Holland).... *Tel 020/638–9398. Entrepotdok 4, bus 22 or 32.*

Studio Theater. Tucked behind the Stadsschouwburg, this tiny place shows occasional English-language gems like *McCabe and Mrs. Miller*.... *Tel 020/625–5454. Lijnbaansgracht 238; tram 1, 2, 5, 6, 7, 10, or 11.*

Tattoo Museum. Almost a modified sales pitch for skin art (this place is the brainchild of Hanky Panky Tattooing), the museums houses an extensive photo library of elaborate tattoos and stages demonstrations with audience participation.... *Tel 020/625–1565. Oudezijds Achterburgwal; tram 4, 9, or 14. Open until 10pm.*

Theater Instituut Nederland. Small neighborhood performing arts space where small-scale classical works are performed in Dutch.... *Tel 020/623–5104. Herengracht 168; tram 1, 2, 5, or 11.*

Torture Museum. Madame Tussaud's in London gives better dungeon than this tourist trap. Even Disney World's Haunted House is way scarier than this parade of shackles, guillotines, racks, and such.... *Tel 020/639–2027. Damrak 20–22; all buses and trams to Centraal Station, Metro Centraal Station. Open daily until 11pm.*

Tropeninstituut. In a past life that began in 1926, this tropical museum was built to showcase the xenophobic Dutch Colonial Institute. Almost fifty years later, the learned house turned its studies toward indigenous people of the tropics. Cultural events in the small Soeterijn performance space—dance, theater, world music, film, and lectures—follow the theme.... *Tel 020/568–8500. Mauritskade 63, tram 9 or 14.*

Tuschinski. A gushy, ornate Dutch art deco movie theater just off Rembrandtplein with an authentic silent movie-era organ—you half expect to see Vincent Price's ghost looking for a seat.... *Tel 020/626–2633. Reguliersbreestraat 26; tram 4, 9, 14, 16, 24, or 25.*

University Theatre. The home of *Caterwauling Company*, a contemporary theater company that often performs in English.... *Tel 020/623–0127; Nieuwe Doelenstraat 16; tram 4, 9, or 14.*

Villa Baranka. Newcomer venue on the classical arts scene that seeks to create a more intimate space for its weekend theater, musical, and spoken-word productions.... *Tel 020/627–6480. Prins Hendrikkade 140; bus 22, 32, 33, 34, 35, 36, or 39.*

Vrieshuis Amerika. An ultra-funky, eight-story underground waterfront squat just east of Centraal Station that resembles a theme-park invisioned by the chemically altered. Inside is a skatepark complete with ramps, a replica of a Wild West American frontier town, a restaurant, an Internet cafe, a performance space, and a makeshift film house.... *Tel 020/668–4252. Oostelijke Handelskade 25; bus 28, 32, or 39.*

Waalse Kerk. Amsterdam's former French Huguenot church, this small, elegant house of worship in the Red Light District hosts chamber music and choral concerts by notable European performers.... *Tel 020/623–2074. Oudezijds Achterburgwal 157; all trams, buses, and Metro to Centraal Station.*

Westerkerk. On the same block as the Anne Frankhuis, this church boasts the tallest tower in Amsterdam. At 272 feet, it's difficult to miss it, partly because it is topped with a gawky replica of the Imperial Crown of Maximilian. Heads up, triviameisters: Rembrandt is buried in this church. Organ recitals are offered year round.... *Tel 020/624–7766. Prinsengracht 281; tram 13, 14, or 17.*

Westergasfabriek. A gas factory recycled into an entertainment complex of bar, restaurant, and performance and exhibition spaces on the western reaches of town. Young, artsy crowds flock here for experimental theater, raves, rock shows by B-team bands, and art gallery openings swarming with like-minded hipsters.... *Tel 020/621–1211. Haarlemmerweg 8–10, bus 18 or 22.*

THE ARTS ♪ THE INDEX

spo

rts

4

Not nearly as sports-
obsessed as North
Americans, the Dutch
can nevertheless get
whipped into a frenzy over
voetball. Even though on
the European scale of

fanaticism Holland doesn't compete with Italy, Spain, and England, soccer is far and away the most popular spectator sport in this country. Amsterdammers turn out in droves to watch **Ajax,** the city's top team and the country's most famous. When Holland met Brazil in the 1994 World Cup—and lost—newspapers here reported that about 75 percent of all the TVs in the country were tuned in. In 1995 when Ajax took the European championship, frenzied fans went ballistic, attacking people on the streets, looting stores, breaking windows, and setting small fires.

Though more Dutch are joining health clubs and jogging, they're still generally a bit nonplussed during discussions of participatory sports and perplexed at the American habit of scheduling time for sports as a means of keeping fit. Bicycle riding and hearty walking are mainstays of daily culture here. Exercise for the Dutch isn't something scheduled; it's woven into everyday life. The biggest perk of going Dutch—and engaging in outdoor sports—in the summertime is the extended daylight: from May until September the sun doesn't set until 10pm.

The biggest participant sport in the Netherlands is bicycling, though most of the Dutch refer to it as transportation. The Tour de France is viewed and rerun and re-rerun on television every summer, and the Dutch equivalent, the **Van Chaam**, a 60-mile race, brings thousands of spectators and hundreds of professional and amateur cyclists to Noord Brabant, a village south of Amsterdam, each August. Other popular participatory sports include tennis (there are public and private courts throughout the city); health clubs and gyms with the same sort of equipment and chrome you'll find back home; and table games like ping-pong, snooker, billiards, and a form of pool called *carambole.*

The Lowdown

Where to watch

Soccer... The 150,000-seat **Amsterdam Arena** (tel 020/
691–2906 for stadium schedules and info, 020/694–6515
for **Ajax** team ticket schedules and information; Amsterdam Zuidoost, Metro Strandvliet), which eerily resembles
the spaceship in *Close Encounters of the Third Kind*, was
inaugurated in August 1996, replacing the smaller
19,000-seat Ajax Stadium. Soccer season runs from
September through June, with a brief exhibition season
that kicks off—literally—in mid-August. Until recently
most games were played in the daytime, but thanks to the
new stadium's monstrous kilowatt capacity, more Ajax
games will now be scheduled in the nocturnal realm. The
fans are a cross-section of the populace—adolescent boys,
families, older folks, children, and the infamous rowdies
that British soccer fans are most known for. The Ajax
audiences appear relatively sedate, but are legendary for
unruliness, shouting, and disturbing the peace enough
that the team was banned from the European football
league in 1990 for a year because of out-of-control crowds.

Batter up... Though the games are not nearly as popular
here as in the States, the city does have a baseball team for
those in need of a fix. If part of the thrill for you is the roar
of the crowd, however, you'll be disappointed by the
attendance and the apathy. The **Pirates** baseball team's
season runs from April through October, and the semi-
pro team is like watching the minor leagues because the
audiences are skimpy, the action isn't polished, and there
are no big names to recognize and ambush for autographs.
The small **Jan van Galenstraat Sportpark** (tel 020/616–
2151; Jan van Galenstraat 316; tram 13, bus 19 or 47)

holds only 2,500 spectators, and the empty seats attest to the Dutch indifference to the sport.

Hoop dreams... Ditto on the indifference for basketball and the local **Canadians Amsterdam** team (tel 020/ 671–3910; Apollohal, Stadionweg; tram 5 or 24, bus 15). Games are played at 8pm every Saturday from October through June to a sparse crowd. The Canadians is part of an inter-Europe league of men's and women's teams of mostly local talent with a couple of imported players from other European countries. Truly sports-minded Amsterdammers (or fans of pro basketball more akin to something the Dream Team would play) are more likely to be home catching a Chicago Bulls game on Euro-sport TV and placing bets on the color of Dennis Rodman's hair.

Where to play

On ice... When winter descends, most Amsterdammers don their skates and Walkmans and take to the frozen canals and ice rinks in public squares; this is when the city looks like so many of those Dutch Master paintings you were forced to stare at in Art History 101. Leidseplein coats with ice by October and becomes the city's makeshift municipal skating rink. Amsterdammers take to the frozen canals as well (beware of skating beneath bridges where the ice takes longer to solidify) and the small ponds in Vondelpark. The best skating advice is to go where you see locals; they are much more versed in gauging the thickness of the ice. Most locals own their skates and the city is almost bereft of rental shops. Try **Jaap Eden Baan** (tel 020/694–9894; Radioweg 64;tram 9, bus 8; open Oct–Mar). For more info about sports events, including where to purchase tickets to basketball, soccer, and baseball games, call the **VVV** (see Down and Dirty) or Amsterdam's **Sport and Recreation Department** (tel 020/522–2490).

Bicycling... In a city where motorists are subordinate to bicyclists, *fietspaden* (bicycle lanes) are plentiful and clearly marked, making this native approach to transportation safe and manageable at night and even for those who have just graduated from training wheels. Traffic signals specifically for bicycles—with bike symbols that flash in green, yellow, and red—attest to how seriously the Dutch take their two-wheelers. Number crunchers posit that there are more than 550,000 bicycles within the city limits (which is just 250,000 shy of Amsterdam's total population). Any time of day, wherever you look, you'll see pedalers in miniskirts, business suits, or outrageous clubwear; balancing groceries, furniture, flowers, briefcases, even a passenger or two. At night thickets of bikes crowd the racks outside clubs, restaurants, and cafes. In the midst of the standard-issue Army green or black models, you'll also spot some tattooed with stripes, polka dots, plastic flowers, neon colors ("so you can pick yours out of the hundreds of others after a night of many beers," one Dutch student said.)

Bike rental companies are scattered around the city. Most require a deposit and a passport for rental. Some rules of the road to keep in mind: Bicyclists are not allowed to travel two abreast; even though the anarchic locals do it, don't follow their lead. Bicycles must have reflector lights on both front and back fenders. And *always* lock your bike, preferably with two locks (most bikes come with a self-lock on the back wheel and rental shops provide an additional U-lock or sturdy chain). Bike theft is rampant in Amsterdam—locals wryly claim that bike stealing is a more popular than bike riding). Witness the skeletal remains of frames, wheels, and ineffective antitheft devices chained to bridges and railings around town. Inquire about bike insurance when you rent; with many companies it's part of the fine print. If the bike is stolen while in your care, you cover the cost.

Also, not every area of town suits bike riding. In the Red Light District narrow, cobblestoned streets and constant crowds make navigation and balance tricky. Tourists thicken the area between Centraal Station and Spui; it's best to navigate both of these areas on foot. But the rest of the city, especially the parks and the outlying areas, are best seen from the seat of a cycle. Sundays, when most Amsterdammers stay home, is the best day of the week for having a leisurely ride without having to play "Dodge the Pedestrians." One insider's note: Don't rent a mountain bike. Riding one is akin to having a neon sign on your forehead that screams, "Tourist."

SPORTS ⟨ THE LOWDOWN

The cheapest rental in town is **Take A Bike** (tel 020/624–8391; Centraal Station, Stationsplein 6; tram 1, 2, 4, 5, 9, 11, 13, 16, 17, 24, or 25; open daily until midnight; Dfl 8 a day (or night) with Dfl 200 deposit), which has a fleet of appropriately dented and tested models that won't mark you immediately as a visitor. The only other rental company open at night is **Stalling Amstel** (tel 020/692–3584; Amstelstation, Julianaplein; Metro Amstelstation; open daily until 10pm; Dfl 10 a day, Dfl 250 deposit).

Billiards, snooker, and *carambole*... The Dutch enjoy playing billiards (*biljart*), but they have their own variation of the gentlemanly sport: *carambole*. Largely a working–class diversion—no tuxedos or dashing rogues with chilled martinis—*carambole* is played on a pocketless table. Chat up a local for the full rundown of rules. Many brown cafes have a table tucked in the back. The most popular of the bona fide *carambole* clubs (with snooker and billiards on the side) is **Biljartcentrum Bavaria** (tel 020/676–4056; Van Ostadestraat 97; tram 3, 12, 24, or 25; open Sun–Thu until 1am, Fri–Sat until 2am; Dfl 10–15 an hour). The scene: Die-hard fanatics whisper tips on strategy in the ears of less-experienced players; the urban uniformed (black on black) drop in after a tony dinner in an arty cafe for a game or two; sports-juiced but perplexed tourists watch intently, trying to decipher the moves. **Snookercentrum de Keizer** (tel 020/623–1586; Keizersgracht 256; tram 13, 14, or 17; open Sun–Thu until 1am, Fri–Sat until 2am; Dfl 9–15) is less of a social scene. Instead, the air here is usually thick with the quiet hum of concentration. There's a lot of nail biting and deep cigarette inhaling on the part of the players hunched over the dozen tables of the **Snooker Center** (tel 020/620–4974; Rokin 28; all trams and buses to Centraal Station; open daily until 11pm; Dfl 13.50–15 per hour). This is serious snooker territory; pros only. The atmosphere at **Snookercentrum de Munt** (tel 020/620–2040; Reguliersbreestraat 16; tram 4, 9, 16, 24, or 25; open Mon–Sat until midnight; Dfl 11–15 per hour) is a bit more easygoing. Around the dozen tables are players exhibiting vastly varying degrees of finesse; there's often someone around who's willing to show beginners the ropes (or the balls, as it were). **Snookerclub Overtoom**

(tel 020/618–8019; Overtoom 209; tram 1, 6, or 11, bus 171 or 172; open Sun–Thu until 1am, Fri–Sat until 2am; Dfl 15 an hour) is housed in a former church. Reverence still pervades the place as players ponder strategy and whisper prayers to unseen deities.

Bowling... If you get an inexplicable itch to wear those goofy shoes and roll big black balls toward a stand of pins while you're in Amsterdam, the only night shop in town is **Knijn Bowling Centre** (tel 020/664–2211; Scheldeplein 3; tram 12 or 25; open Mon–Sat until 1am, Sun until 11pm; Dfl 26–39 per hour). It's got 22 lanes, disco music, and that standard-issue bowling alley atmosphere (read: it's a gathering place for life's flotsam and jetsam and fugitives from the fashion police).

Jogging... Amsterdam presents its own unique hazards and distractions for joggers. For one thing, uneven cobblestoned surfaces vex even the most sure-footed runners. Add to that the fact that most streets are narrow and sidewalks are crowded. Then of course trams, busses, pedestrians, bicycles, and cars share the roadway and (oddly enough) seem to conspire to interrupt the lope, the rhythm, the zen. As if that weren't enough, blue clouds of hash smoke drift from storefronts, providing potentially lethal distraction from the health-minded chore at hand. That being said, the city's parks are really the best place for a run. **Vondelpark** (in the Old South neighborhood just beyond Singlegracht and near big musuems; main entry is on Stadhouderskade; tram 1, 2, 3, 5, 6, 7, 10, or 12) in the city center is flush with pre-dinner hour joggers, and on the southern edge of the city runners flatten their Nikes in **Amsterdamse Bos** (on the southern edge of town; main entry on Amstelveenseweg; bus 170, 171, 172), where distances are marked with signposts. In May the **Amsterdam Marathon** snakes its way 42 kilometers through the city (see **Festivals** in the Down and Dirty chapter for more details).

Gambling... Wagering is not the sport of choice in Amsterdam. Betting the ponies and puppies is not a happening thing, and legal casinos are scarce, gaudy, and imbued with a sticky sort of lounge-lizard feel. The swankiest place to roll the dice is **Holland Casino** (tel 020/620–

SPORTS ⏋ THE LOWDOWN

1006; Max Euweplein 62; tram 1, 2, 5, 6, 7, 10, or 11; open daily until 3am; Dfl 5 cover, jacket required for men, minimum age 18). It's mostly a hairpiece-and-sequin kind of crowd, occasionally augmented by a busload of tourists desperately seeking Monte Carlo. If betting is a cog in the wheel of your mental health, the only option is to wager on the ponies—the British horse races, that is—at **Totalisator** (tel 020/622–9198; Lange Niezel 12; tram 4, 9, 16, 24, or 25; and tel 020/623–8583; Leidestraat 101; tram 1, 2, 5, or 11; both open daily until 8pm).

Squash and tennis... To play tennis in Amsterdam you'll most likely have to settle for an indoor court; the outdoor courts around the city are for members only. The ten courts inside **Gold Star Tennis** (tel 020/644–5483; K. Lotsylaan 20, Buitenveldert; Metro Buitenveldert; open daily in summer until 11pm; Dfl 25 per hour) are filled with what looks like the cast of a Benetton ad decked out in summer whites. It's very popular in summer, so it might be best to reserve a court. At **Frans Otten Stadion** (tel 020/662–8767; Stadionstraat 10; tram 6 or 24; open Mon–Fri until 11pm, Sat–Sun until 8pm; tennis Dfl25 per hour, squash Dfl 18, racket rental available), the 20 squash courts are usually more in demand than the five tennis courts. The dress code is relaxed, and if you're not at Graff or Agassi level (and don't aspire to be), don't sweat it: most of the racket wielders here aren't, either. The cheapest tennis courts in town are the nine government-subsidized courts at **Kadoelen** (tel 020/631–3194; Kadoelenweg, opposite 230; bus 92; open daily until midnight; Dfl 25 per hour). At **Squash City** (tel 020/626–7883; Ketelmarkerstraat 6; bus 18 or 22; open Mon–Fri until 11:15pm, Sat–Sun until 9pm; Dfl 35 for one hour of court time, major credit cards accepted), a sauna is included in the payment for court time. And if your squash stroke needs help and you have time, instructions are available in English. Don't venture near **Dickey-squash** (tel 020/646–2266; Karel Lotsylaan 16; Metro Zuid, bus 48 or 63; open Mon–Sat until midnight, Sun until 11pm; Dfl 15 for 30 minutes) if you're a novice. Anything less than play-to-maim squash isn't tolerated. Serious squash players rule in this clean, modern complex of courts.

Gyms and saunas... The Dutch don't worship at the altar of the health club as many North Americans do; they can live perfectly happily without a daily StairMaster fix or step class. Exercise, according to one wry Dutch journalist, is not an activity you add onto your life, it is something that you incorporate into your life—witness the Dutch devotion to bicycle riding as a means of everyday transportation. Still, there are some gyms and health clubs here. Most are smaller than their U.S. counterparts and don't have the variety of metallic equipment many regard as staples of the gym scene. Though not advertised as such, **Garden Gym** (tel 020/626–8772; Jodenbreestraat 158, tram 9 or 14; open Mon–Fri until 11pm; Dfl 21.50 for a day pass) is primarily a women's health club featuring weight training, aerobics, massage, self-defense classes, a sauna, and a solarium. Men won't be turned away, but they just may be a bit uncomfortable with the high estrogen levels. **Splash** (tel 020/624–8404; Looiersgracht 26, tram 7 or 10; open Mon–Fri until 10pm; Dfl 25 for a day pass with all classes included; AmEx and Visa accepted) is co-ed, with a yuppie clientele that pumps iron in gender-separated weight rooms or crowds into eight daily aerobic and step classes. During the summer, the club throws open its blue shutters so you can focus on the canal while you count the kilometers on your treadmill. Massage, sauna, and a Turkish bath are included in the day-pass price. Very busy between 5 and 7pm. The leotards are more discreetly cut and you'll notice more thinning hair and thickening waistlines at the **Sporting Club Leidseplein** (tel 020/620–6631; Korte Leidsedwarsstraat 18; tram 1, 2, 5, 6, 7, 10, or 11; open Mon–Fri until midnight; Dfl 25 for a day pass). Imbued with a YMCA-ish feel, the club has a weight room, tanning booths, and sauna. **De Stokerij** (tel 020/625–9417; Rozendwarsstraat 8; tram 13, 14, or 17; open Mon–Sat until 10pm; Dfl 3 an hour) is strictly no-frills. No throbbing disco tunes, no posing, no cruising. The gym has the quaint aroma of years of accumulated perspiration, and the showers are a bit dicey, hygienically speaking. Most come here to use the tennis and volleyball courts. For aerobics classes grunted in English, try the reserved but trendy **H '88** (tel 020/638–0650; Herengracht 88; tram 6, 10, or 11; open daily until 10pm; fees vary), which is popular with expats and assorted internationals. For more passive perspira-

THE LOWDOWN

SPORTS

tion—say you want to skip the workout and head right into the sauna—try **Sauna Damrak** (tel 020/622–6012; Damrak 54, all trams and buses to Centraal Station; open daily until 9pm; Dfl 27.50 with towels) for purging and perspiring. The facility is co-ed and the enlightened European attitude toward nudity prevails, which means next to no lingering looks from your fellow unclothed. The most luxurious sauna in the city is **Deco** (tel 020/623–8215; Herengracht 115; tram 1, 2, 5, 11, 16, 24, or 25; open Mon–Sat until 11pm; Dfl 24), which has resplendent art deco decor, even in the sauna and steam bath. Afterward, sidle up to the cafe for an herb tea or a high–octane wheat drink (a k a beer). You have to go past the waterfall and the Japanese tea garden to get to the even more serene rooftop sauna and terrace of the stylish New Age complex **Oibibio** (tel 020/553–9355; Prins Hendrikkade 20–21; tram 1, 2, 4, 5, 9, 11, 13, 17, or 24, Metro Centraal Station; sauna open daily until midnight; Dfl 25). Next to nil on the attitude scale, the prevailing vibes here are calm and inviting. Sauna use peaks during the early evening hours—try it as a post-dinner/pre-club interlude to recharge yourself for a night on the town.

Chess... The Dutch call them *schaak cafés*, chess taverns where the hard-core king and queen pushers congregate. The chessboard hanging outside the canalfront store in Jordaan signals the activity inside **Gambit** (no phone; Bloemgracht 20; tram 10; open daily until midnight). Plants lined up against the windowpanes form a make-shift curtain and insulate the earnest players in the smoke-filled interior from sidewalk distractions. The pealing bells of Westerkerk provide a musical soundtrack every fifteen minutes. Though chessboards predominate on the tables of **Schaak Café Het Hok** (tel 020/626–2223; Lange Leidsedwarstraat 134; tram 1, 2, 5, or 11; open daily until midnight) people (mostly men) also huddle around games of backgammon, hoisting draughts and betting on winners. In the midst of the tourist–satu-rated bars and restaurants of the area, Het Hok is pri-marily a locals' joint.

In the swim... Even though it's water, water everywhere in Amsterdam, don't venture near the canals for a swim (or, God forbid, fishing) unless you have an unmanageable

Jesus complex. Army tank green, the canals are awash in potent bacteria: streetcleaners sweep debris into the drink, men use them as urinals, and some houseboats empty their septic tanks into the toxic swirl. Annually, the city cops haul at least a corpse or two from their watery graves as well. Swimming in a city canal would be akin to taking a leisurely dip in a vat of acid. You wanna get wet, take it inside. The schedules of indoor swimming pools fluctuate; at most facilities different hours are earmarked for family swimming, adults only, nude swimming, and kiddie lessons. If you're interested in swimming laps, ask about *banen zwemmen*. On the southeastern side of the city, it's faux beach-o-rama at **De Mirandabad** (tel 020/642–8080 or 020/644–6637; De Mirandalaan 9; tram 11, 14, or 22; open Mon–Fri until 10pm; Dfl 5.75 for adults, Dfl 4.50 for kids) with a wave machine, an erstwhile stone beach, whirlpools, water slides, and indoor and outdoor pools (the alfresco Olympic-sized pool is open May through September daily until 9pm). A favorite haunt of families, the decibel level soars with kiddie shrieks and squeals. The **Zuiderbad** (tel 020/679–2217; Hobbemastraat 26; tram 1, 2, or 5, bus 26, 66, 67, 170, or 179; open Mon–Fri until 9pm; Dfl 4.50) is the city's oldest and most architecturally ornate pool. Built in 1912 and renovated in 1994, the grand indoor pool—complete with mosaics, sculptures, painted tiles, and dramatic arches—would make a perfect setting for an Esther Williams flick. **Marnixbad** (tel 020/625–4843; Marnixplein 9; tram 3, 7, or 10; open Wed–Fri until 10pm; Dfl 4.25) sports an entryway fountain with two children shooting water from their mouths. Inside, it's Kid Central, with an 82-foot pool crowned with water slides and a whirlpool. Several of the city's outdoor pools have varying night swimming hours in summer. Phone for prices and times: **Breduisbad** (tel 020/682–9116; Spaarndammerdijk 306; bus 22 or 28) has high-diving platforms and lanes marked for lap swimming; and **Flevoparkbad** (tel 020/692–5030; Zeeburgerdijk 360, tram 14) offers two pools with separate kiddie swim areas and a playground.

Ping pong... Referred to here as table tennis, this quicksilver sport is becoming more popular in Amsterdam. Witness the crowded tables at the city's two table tennis centers. You might expect a place with a name like **Table Tennis**

SPORTS ⟨ THE LOWDOWN

Insitute Amsterdam (tel 020/624–5780; Keizersgracht 209; tram 13, 14, or 17; open daily until 1am; Dfl 10 per table per hour) to feel a little like a formal training school for the sport. Not at all—this place is a wall-to-wall frat party, complete with lots of Bronx cheers, spontaneous whooping, and the general rowdiness of the young and the restless. An equal-opportunity venue, the pros ping and pong here beside the not-so-pro. If you get thirsty you can move to the bar, and if you get sweaty you can head for the showers. The hourly rate at **Tafelcentrum Leoos** (tel 020/624–2287; Marnixplantsoen 1; tram 3, 7, or 10; open Mon–Fri until 1am; Dfl 9 per table per hour) is a guilder cheaper. Here the action rages on into the wee hours with a mixed-age crowd and the sweet smell of hashish in the air.

Laser games... Is it aerobic if it elevates your pulse? While laser games don't officially qualify as a sport, they inspire the same sort of devotion, spirit, and playfulness. At **Intersphere** (tel 020/622–4808; Prins Hendrikkade 190; bus 22, 32, 33, 34, 35, 36, or 39; open Sun–Thu until midnight, Fri–Sat until 1am; Dfl 15 for first 15 mins, Dfl10 for 20 mins thereafter) and **The Force** (tel 020/633–1140; Orange Vrijstaatkade 21; tram 9, bus 59, 120, or 126; open Mon–Thu until midnight, Fri–Sat until 1am; Dfl 15 for 20 minutes) Roy Rogers meets Darth Vader as patrons step into blackened rooms that resemble caves and don belts and holsters for laser guns that jag neon–colored light streams like psychedelic pick-up sticks against the blackness. Frequented by men most likely to be accused of arrested development and a pro-nounced prediliction for juvenilia.

Tee time... Still primarily the domain of the turned-up nose set, golf is nevertheless gaining popularity, most likely because it is beamed into Dutch homes via Eurosport TV and the BBC. Private courses are just that, and you're unlikely to be granted entrance unless you're with a member, most of whom are descended from a line of royalty. Two public courses are available to visiting duffers. Billed as Europe's largest driving range, **Golf en Conference Center Amstelborgh** (tel 020/697–5000; Borchlandweg 6, Metro Bijlmer; open Mon–Fri until 10:30pm, Sat–Sun until 9pm; call for greens fees and tee times) is one. Lit at night, it has a nine-hole course, locker rooms, and a restaurant. The other public course, **Spaarnwoude**, is open at night only in summer (tel 023/338–5599; Het Hogeland 2, bus 176 or 179; open daily in summer until 9pm; Dfl 36 per round at 18-hole course). Wind and water hazards challenge golfers on the 18-, 12-, and nine-hole courses.

In-line skating... This sport o' the moment in most other urban centers faces two insurmountable hazards in Amsterdam, namely cobblestone streets and bikes. If you opt to skate, the bike lanes are usually the most smoothly paved, but dodging the nonstop streams of bikers may test your patience. Skating through Vondelpark and Amsterdamse Bos, two city parks, are your best bet. Check with the guys at **Rodolfo's** (tel 020/622–5488, Sarphatistraat 59, tram 9 or 14; and tel 020/623–1214, Magna Plaza, Nieuwezijds Voorburgwal, tram 1, 2, 5, 11, 13, or 17; Dfl 15 per day with deposit of Dfl 300 or credit card), a cool rental shop with two outlets that claims to be the oldest European skate shop. All the employees are skaters who can turn you on to off-the-beaten paths and local skate parties and clubs (see The Club Scene).

SPORTS ⟨ THE LOWDOWN

hangi

ng out

5

Hanging out in Amsterdam means going native. Any resoundingly vivid visit to the city of the 7,000 gables includes a fair amount of hanging out. Not a passive or static exercise, it means mild engagement. Think strolling and window-shopping. Cruising the canals at dusk, meandering over bridges with arches trimmed in white lights. Gazing at regal 17th-century architecture dramatic in the light of street lamps. Or drinking beer in a sidewalk cafe and people-watching.

The Dutch are endearingly casual, a quality that naturally begets a copious amount of hanging out, and they do it most at sidewalk cafes, where hours are spent talking, debating, writing, eating, drinking, smoking, laughing, and watching the world pass by. Some of the most popular cafes are **Café Americain** in Leidseplein (there are about 1,000 cafe seats on this boisterous square), **Café de Jaren** on the Amstel River, **Café Vertigo** in Vondelpark, and **Café Luxembourg** on Spui.

To get your bearings in the city, remember that the innermost city is where all the canals are; and it's divided into two areas, each with its own landmark church, the **Oude Zijde** (Old Side), on the east, and the **Nieuwe Zijde** (New Side), on the west. Within Oude Zijde is the **Red Light District**, the oldest section of the town that today proffers the world's oldest profession. **Waterlooplein** is the site of a daily flea market and the Stadhuis Muziektheater (Stopera), the white modern structure that houses the government and the arts. There's also **Nieuwmarkt**, housing the city's Chinatown and old Jewish Quarter. Bounded by the Amstel and the streets Oudezijds Voorburgwal, Nieuwe Herengracht, and Prins Hendrikkade, this neighborhood's beacon is the Oude Kerk, the oldest church in Amsterdam.

The western half of the innermost city center is the **Nieuwe Zijde** (New Side), which encompasses **Centraal Station**, **Damrak**, site of the Koninklijk Paleis; Kalverstraat, the city's main shopping street; and the **Nieuwe Kerk** built to accommodate overflow churchgoers that the Oude Kerk could no longer accommodate. The New Side is bounded by the Singel canal to the west and south, Oudezijds Voorburgwal on the east, and Centraal Station to the north.

West of the Singel and the New Side is the **Western Canal Ring**, a section of town that encompasses **Jordaan**, a bohemian neighborhood of galleries, restaurants, and lofts. **Westerkerk** stands as the tallest point in this neighborhood that is bounded by Rozengracht on the south, Het IJ on the north, Singel Gracht on the west, and the Singel on the east.

South of the Western Canal Ring and the New Side is the **Central Canal Ring** where tourists throng to **Leidse-**

plein, a bustling square bounded by shops and restaurants catering to travelers. The most heavily visited tourist areas are also found just east of this district in the **Eastern Canal Ring**, home of **Rembrandtplein**, another heavily neoned square; **Albert Cuypmarkt**, the city's most popular daily street market; and **Bloemenmarkt**, the floating flower market on the Singel west of Muntplein.

The **Museum Quarter** is the most southern area in the city center. It houses **Vondelpark**, the city's equivalent to Central Park, and the Holy Trinity of Amsterdam museums: **the Rijksmuseum**, the **Van Gogh museum**, and the **Stedelijk**.

The most eastern wedge of town is called **Plantage**, the plantation parkland that was once beyond the city wall. Today it is primarily residential, although visitors venture there to see **Artis**, the city's zoo; the **Planetarium**; and the **Koninklijk Theater Carré**, the ornate concert hall that once housed the city's circus.

Visitors shouldn't miss out on the sights they will discover by walking around the four concentric city center canals (**Singel**, **Herengracht**, **Keizersgracht**, and **Prinsengracht**): gabled rooftops, the hidden courtyards the Dutch call *hofjes*, the engraved cartouches on housefronts that used to identify inhabitants by their profession, bridges, boats, and water, water everywhere.

The Lowdown

Views from above... Though only open Thursday evenings until 9:30pm (the rest of the week the doors shut promptly at 6pm), the **sixth-floor cafe at Metz & Co.** (tel 020/624–8810; Keizersgracht 455; tram 1, 2, 5, or 11), a posh but accessible department store, offers an above-the-rooftops view hard to come by in this sea-level city. When it was completed in 1891, the building was, in fact, the tallest in Amsterdam. Capped with a cupola and perched on regal Keizersgracht just off the popular and tourist-riddled Leidsestraat, the store sells Neiman Marcus-esque goods (but foregoes the snooty attitude) on five floors. One floor up, the cafe's selection is a bit pricey and upscale. If you're really hungry but on a budget, go for a Metzburger; otherwise eschew the food, order a *koffie verkeerd* (literally, incorrect coffee, a weak blend of espresso and steamed milk), hold hands with a loved one, and think deep, Continental thoughts as you survey the rooftops and ruckus below.

Among the assorted New Age restaurants, bookstores, cafes, and centers dotting Amsterdam's relentlessly picturesque streets, the New Age emporium-*cum*-minimall **Oibibio** (tel 020/553–9355; Prins Hendrikkade 20–21; tram 1, 2, 4, 5, 9, 11, 13, 16, 17, 24, or 25; Metro Centraal Station) feels almost like crunchy corporate counterculture with its art deco murals, its stylish clientele, and its cruelty-free goods and services: a Japanese tea garden, a book and CD store, a center for lectures and classes, a gourmet vegetarian restaurant, and—drumroll, please—*a sauna with rooftop terrace* (Dfl 26). Open daily until midnight, the terrace is a hidden jewel in the city center that offers dynamic high-rise views. After you heat-purge the hedonistic poisons of Amsterdam in a coed Finnish sauna or Turkish steam room, it offers a whiff of bracing night air and a visual sweep of a city most see only from ground level.

On the waterfront... Akin to the *bateaux mouches* that ply the Seine in Paris (but minus the hyper-wattage klieg lights), scores of enclosed canal boats snake through Amsterdam's waterways providing canned commentary in a U.N. assortment of languages. A cheesy experience, to be sure, especially when you queue behind coveys of bus tourists. Evening tours offer gastronomically insulting cheese and wine, and some even include a stop at an "authentic" bar, which is usually anything but. And yet there is no more fitting way to see this city of 200 canals, 1,281 bridges, and 2,500 houseboats—especially at night, when white lights illuminate the arched bridges and buildings like some EPCOT version of Euro-perfection.

Almost two dozen boat operators offer night cruises, with the quality among the most popular almost indistinguishable. The primary embarkation points are opposite Centraal Station and along Rokin. **Holland International** (tel 020/622–7788; departs opposite Centraal Station; tram 1, 2, 4, 5, 9, 11, 13, 16, 17, 24, or 25; Metro Centraal Station; night cruise 9:30pm nightly, reservations required, Dfl 42.50; dinner cruise 8pm, Tue, Thur–Sat, reservations required, Dfl 135; major credit cards accepted) is the biggie of the boat tours, particularly popular with camera-toting older folks who travel in busloads and wear socks with their sandals. The dinner cruise offers a four-course meal no more threatening than a Rotary luncheon and covers the basic Chamber-of-Commerce points of interest. **Lovers** (tel 020/622–2181; Prinsen Hendrikkade by Centraal Station; tram 1, 2, 4, 5, 9, 11, 13, 16, 17, 24, or 25; Metro Centraal Station; 9:30pm cruise nightly, reservations required, Dfl 39; major credit cards accepted) with its two-hour, candlelit ride, is usually chosen by the romantically inclined. For the "Lifestyles of the Rich and Famous" boat tour, book one of the four boats from **The Marina** (tel 020/676–3569; Hilton Marina, Apollolaan 138-140; tram 5 or 24; wide range of rates for charters). Each boat is trés fashionable—stocked liquor cabinets, fireplaces, antique trim and decor, Vanna White-esque hostesses, and salty captains who look like escapees from Old Spice commercials. The *Leifde* (love), with delft tiles, wood-burning stove, etched

HANGING OUT ⟆ THE LOWDOWN

glass, mahogany trim, and just-so antiques, looks as if Martha Stewart had a hand in its decoration. Less bullying on the budget are **Canal Buses**, 52-seater boats that are the newest addition to the city's public transportation system. The fleet operates until 10pm in the summertime and makes 30-minute loops from the Rijksmuseum to Centraal Station, with stops at Leidseplein, Keizersgracht, and Westerkerk (tel 020/623–9886; Weteringschans 24; tram 6 or 10; Dfl 15 for a day ticket, Dfl 22 for two-day pass).

Another way to get around via canal is in those odd contraptions locals call *waterfiets* (water bikes) and rental agencies dub *pedalos* (It's a bike! It's a boat!... It's a boke?). Pedaling a two- or four-seater along the canals is a good way to burn off the carbos from a *rijsttafel* dinner or an afternoon sampling the city's high-octane wheat drinks. You may have to endure some snickering from the locals, however. **Watersport Roell** (tel 020/692–9124; Mauritskade 1, by the Amstel; tram 6, 7, or 10; open until 10pm Tue–Sat, Apr–Sept; Dfl 17.50 per hour for two-seater, Dfl 26 per hour for four-seater) is the only one of the city's water bike shops that remains open in the evening. If you take the bait, don't let the precious little white lights outlining the bridges mesmerize: You'll need to keep your wits about you to dart away from the big canal boats hogging the waterways and broadcasting canned factoids at their blue-haired passengers.

Bridging the gap... Madison County pilgrims, take note: Statisticians who thrive on compiling such data put the number of Amsterdam bridges at 1,281, spanning 160 canals and rivers. Dozens, even hundreds, will be traversed by any visitor who navigates this city, but several are worth a visit and perhaps a Kodak moment. Inspired by Paris' Pont Alexandre III, the **Blauwebrug**, which spans the Amstel and links Amstelstraat with Waterlooplein, is one of the city's most elaborate trans-waterway constructions. Ornate and rococo, it speaks of fading glamour.

It didn't take a Rhodes scholar to conjure the nickname of the famed Skinny Bridge, or **Magerebrug**, which links Kerkstraat and Nieuwekerkstraat, and was built in the 17th century at the whim of two lazy sisters who lived on opposite sides of the Amstel and didn't want to walk around it. One of eight wooden bridges in the city, it rots out every twenty years or so, is regularly refurbished, and is still cranked by hand when boats pass underneath. For an even skinnier bridge, minus the billing, hoof it to the **Westerdok** neighborhood, west of Centraal Station. The **Drieharingbrug** (Three Herrings Bridge), which connects the western end of Prinseneiland to Realeneiland, is both thinner and more picturesque than the Skinny Bridge. Finally, for illuminated poetry and a spot that screams romance, go to **Reguliersgracht where it crosses Keizersgracht**: Your vista will include a view of 15 bridges, all outlined at night by hundreds of white lights. (To take them all in at once, you have to swivel your head 360 degrees, *Exorcist*-style.) Kissing is imperative, swooning recommended, and those wide sighs that signal simultaneous longing and contentment will undoubtedly well forth.

Fun stuff for free... Outside Centraal Station on **Stationsplein** is where you'll probably first encounter street music: stringy-haired sitarists, violinists, Andean pipe bands, someone massacring a Beatles tune on the guitar, harmonica players, the pipe organ players who grind out "He married the girl with the strawberry curl and the band played on" while shaggy guys with tin cans rattle coins to the beat. Like most large European cities, Amsterdam draws street musicians, buskers, and performers trolling for crowds possibly willing to fork over a spare guilder or two. If you like this sort of entertainment, you can find more in the **Leidseplein**, where decent-sized crowds circle agile young men who can juggle flaming bowling pins, fit their big bodies into small boxes, or swallow swords. The occasional string quartet also sets up, lending a genteel, FM quality to the honky-tonk of the square. If you want a haunting and memorable street music experience, try **the archway beneath the Rijksmuseum on Museumkade**. On some nights a sax player roosts there in the early evening hours. He blows soulful, bluesy riffs, and the acoustics make the sound swell and echo like nobody's business. **Vondelpark**, named for Dutch poet Joost van den Vondel, provides a pastoral, albeit crowded, backdrop for both amateur musicians and pros. During the summer, free concerts there are sponsored at the *Openluchttheater* (check with the VVV for details). Mimes, mannequins, and singers prefer the wide

HANGING OUT ⟍ THE LOWDOWN

sidewalks of **Damrak**, while some of the city's lesser musicians have been known to serenade Metro riders with selections like "Stairway to Heaven" or classic Dutch drinking songs. Your choices are feigning deafness, averting your eyes, or coughing up some change to chase the noise away. Should you prefer to travel by boat at night anyway, the **ferry ride across the IJ River** is itself a cost-free diversion. From Pier 7 behind Centraal Station, the *Buikerslotervegveer* ferry operates 24 hours a day, making quick round-trip treks to Amsterdam Noord, a lackluster suburb.

For evening window-shopping, avoid Kalverstraat and P.C. Hooftstraat, two popular shopping streets where closing time means rolling metal security gates over the windows. Instead, some of the city's best windowlust is savored among the antique stores around the **Spiegelgracht** and on **Nieuwe Spiegelstraat**. Perhaps inspired by the Rijksmuseum—lit in its glory just a block south of the Spiegelgracht—these shop displays are like minimuseums. Windows overflow with maps, etchings, vases, antique jewelry, velvet and brocades, and artfully arranged *objets* that look as if posed for a Rembrandt still life.

Tilting at windmills... Though the windmill is one of the country's most exported images, Amsterdam is not the primo sighting spot (the town **De Zaanse Schans**, about nine miles north, is the best place to ooh and aah at the icons at work). There are six windmills in the city, five of which are private homes or shops that deny access at night. But the fanciful structures inspire pilgrimages and some are lit dramatically in the evening. The most photoworthy is **De Rieker**, on the Amstel river behind Amstel Park (Amsteldijk near De Borcht; bus 148). If you deem it worthy of capturing artistically (even on your disposable camera), you'll be in memorable company: Rembrandt painted here and the windmill was said to be his muse. The 18th-century **De Gooyer** windmill, also called *Funenmolen*, is now home to the **Bierbrouwerij 't IJ**, an independent microbrewery (see The Bar and Cafe Scene for more details) with stellar brews and the maddening closing time of 8:30pm. A former corn mill, it stands sentinel over the Nieuwevaart canal east of Centraal Station.

A little night music... Cherubim and seraphim no doubt cavort during summer months in the lofty interior of **de Nieuwe Kerk**, at the corner of Dam Square, when the church hosts its series of Sunday evening organ concerts. Amsterdam boasts 42 church organs and this one, built in 1645, is a towering, regal series of pipes adorned by gilded angels and potbellied cherubs. Concerts begin at 8pm and last an hour; tickets are Dfl 12.50 and available from the AUB ticket-booth on Leidseplein and at the door at show time.

For vidiots... With all the understatement of a Vegas casino, two honky-tonk, neon-blitzed video-game parlors spill their kilowatts onto the Damrak just a pinball's roll away from Centraal Station. **Carrousel Arcade BV Amusements** (tel 020/624–613; Damrak 62; open until midnight daily) and **Macau Amusementpaleis** (no phone; Damrak 15; open until midnight daily) are both ablaze with video games, pinball machines, and assorted electronic playground games. The mostly male and unshaven crowds wear sunglasses at night and look as if they moonlight as Meatloaf roadies.

Where to spot wildlife... We're not talking Marlin Perkins in the *veldt*—Amsterdam nocturnal wildlife leans toward the bizarrely bedecked, the outrageously ornamented, and the curiously coiffed.

The most interesting people-watching has got to be the young clubgoers who begin to venture out at about midnight. Lime-green, spiked hair. Three men in red lipstick dressed like college professors. Pierced everything. Teetering wedges in neon colors. Jungle-print leggings on both genders. Black trousers, shirts, bad posture. Industrio-urban shoes and fat heels for women; hang-tough, Doc Marten-ish numbers for the men. The hives for nighttime crowds are **Rembrandtplein** (truly scary people on the make, people who travel in packs, a guy who draws caricatures, the glare of competitive neon); **Leidseplein** (heavy on the buskers and grungo-hip backpackers, 1,000 sidewalk cafe seats), **Spui** (anarchy lite, yuppies in suits, good food); **Jordaan** (a Dutch version of New York's SoHo); and **the Red Light District** (storefront hookers bathed in red neon, drunken and fixated men, bobbing Japanese tourists).

THE LOWDOWN

HANGING OUT

Late-night shopping (and shoe fetishes)... During the 17th century, Amsterdam was the mercantile capital of the world (read: shopping central) and that legacy continues in the city's abundance of large department stores, el cheapo outlet stores, one-of-a-kind designer boutiques, and specialty shops that each delight in niche needs as narrow as buttons, toothbrushes, wallets, or tea. But, simply put, most of your mass consuming is best left to regular business hours. The shops that line the streets and taunt you with promises of clothing, shoes, leather goods, books, cosmetics, and diamonds all close daily at 6pm, except for one blessed night of the week, Thursday, which the Dutch call *koopavond* (shopping night), when a good assortment stay open until 9. If you brake for shoe stores, if some of your closest pals are Kenneth Cole and Joan and David, if a shoehorn is music to your feet (you get the idea), **Panama**, on the aptly named P.C. Hooftstraat (tel 020/622–1908; P.C. Hooftstraat 124; tram 2, 3, 5, or 12; open Thur until 9pm), sells hip and empowering shoes for women who are old enough to never again be carded but young enough to harbor the wish that they would be. Just down the street is another shrine to female footwear, **Shoebaloo**, (tel 020/671–2210; P.C. Hooftstraat 80; tram 2, 3, 5, or 12; open Thur until 9) with a selection heavy on the black, industrial-chic look and popular with twenty- and thirtysomethings.

Browsing for books and CDs... If you feel the need for some quiet browsing and scoping, the multilevel **American Book Center** (tel 020/625–5537; Kalverstraat 185; trams 4, 9, 14, 16, or 24; open Mon–Sat until 10pm) stocks everything you'd find in Waldenbooks for about the same price. The international art magazine section (primo meeting territory) is home to hipsters of every stripe poring over those glossy pages. A short stroll away at central Spui is **Athenaeum Boekhandel** (tel 020/622–6248; Spui 14–16; tram 1, 2, 5, or 11; open Thur until 10), a hang-out of Amsterdam literati. It looks and feels like the hippest bookstore in an American university town like Ann Arbor or Berkeley. The healthy selection of English titles lures the intellectual expat crowd as well, and the friendly staff is well-versed in the city's highbrow exhibits and activities. You won't get the menacing management eyeball if you park on the floor and read for a couple of hours.

Do you absolutely need to own that ska tune you heard in a club at four o'clock last night? For world music, it's **Musiques du Monde** (tel 020/624–1354; Singel 281; tram 1, 2, 5, or 11; open Thur until 9pm), where a faint blue haze of tobacco and incense smoke hangs over the racks of world tune CDs and tapes. Listening booths allow you to sample before you plunk down your guilders.

Flower power... The Dutch exhibit a fondness for fresh flowers and corner vendors crank up the color voltage on the gray urban streets. To sate floral urges or to assimilate into Dutch culture—flowers are customary when visiting friends—**Moonflower** (tel 020/627–1133; Centraal Station; all trams to Centraal Station, Metro Centraal Station; open until 9 daily) stocks bouquets of varying plumage and, yes, tulips.

Nightshops... The city's *avondwinkel* (nightshops) are designed to stay open until 1am, but they stock mainly consumable items and necessities like toothpaste, toilet paper, candy bars, and not-in-mixed-company personal hygiene products, usually at shriek-inducing prices. But it's Economics 101: If you've gotta have, you're gonna pay, right? **Dolf's Avondverkoop** (tel 020/625–9503; Willemsstraat 79; tram 3; open until 1am daily) in the Jordaan is a late-night lifesaver, if you are in panic-driven need of drugstore items and snacks bearing a tentative resemblance to any of the four known food groups. For first-class food urges, the more pedigreed the better (say, a dozen oysters on the half shell and a chilled split of Veuve Cliquot), ring first at **Heuft's First Class Night-shop** (tel 020/642–4048; Rijnstraat 62; tram 4 or 25; open until 1am daily). Heuft's stocks delicacies both imported and homegrown and delivers to your doorstep.

Tobacco and chocolate... For the kind of smokable substances that won't get you flagged at customs, the most elegant tobacconist in the city is **P.G.C. Hajenuis** (tel 020/623–7494; Rokin 96; tram 4, 9, 14, 16, 24, or 25; open Thur until 9), housed in an appropriately clubby and gentlemanly building (circa 1915) on Rokin. A chandelier dominates the red interior, which is bedecked with marble and wood paneling. They'll ship tobacco and assorted accoutrements anywhere. And whatever you do—inhale.

HANGING OUT ⟍ THE LOWDOWN

The herbal culture of the city can lead, some say, to a serious sweet tooth—refined sugar in gastroporno-graphic configurations is the only answer. **Jordino** (tel 020/420–3225; Haarlemmerdijk 25a, bus 18 or 22; open Mon–Sat until 10), a slick little store near the Shipping Quarter section of town, handmakes all its treats: marzi-pan-swaddled walnuts, chocolate-covered coffee beans, whipped cream splats entombed in dark chocolate, and ice cream that could inspire that insipid chant we all barked as children, "I scream, you scream, we all scream for ice cream!"

Adult toys for girls and boys... Interspered with store-front prostitutes, sleazy sex shows and cinemas, smoking coffeeshops, slimy hawkers, and oily bars of the Red Light District are dozens of sex toy shops with window displays that would coax the Christian Coalition into a coronary attack. It's cross-merchandising at its basest level: suggestive food, mammary-oriented magazines, videos, lubricants, vibrators—you get the idea. Unfortunately, the classiest stores of the lot—Absolute Danny, Mail and Female—don't have evening hours. Still, if you are compelled to buy a souvenir as you stroll past the red-neon-bathed hookers, you can heed the call at the sex shops on the seedier side of town, which are open until the wee hours. But you're on your own in the Red Light District. For the same salacious goods at lower prices, venture out of the District. In De Pijp, **Blue and White** (tel 020/610–1741; Ceintuurbaan 248; tram 3, 12, 24, or 25; open Thur until 9pm) has bargain bins (Attention, K-Mart shoppers, it's a blue-light special!!), discount videos, memorable toys, cheapo Euro-versions of *Playboy, Penthouse*, and books in excessively poor taste. **The Bronx** (tel 020/623–1548; Kerkstraat 53-55; tram 1, 2, 5, or 11) is a gay sex-toy shop, open until midnight daily, that stocks lots of porno videos starring buffed studs in hard hats and lotsa leather accoutrements. Party on, Wayne. Party on, Garth.

Fetish clothing... For men or women who desire to be laced into leather or wrapped in rubber, **Demask** (tel 020/620–5603; Zeedijk 64; tram 4, 9, 14, 16, 24, or 25; open Thur until 9pm) carries costly bondage wear, collars, slutty boots, S/M gear, and anything else Helmut Newton could possibly need for a photo shoot. **RoB**

Gallery (tel 020/625–4686; Weteringschans 253; tram 6, 7, or 10; open Thur until 9) offers the same sorts of goods—at higher prices—for men only. Well-heeled gays frequent this place for custom-made leather and rubber-wear. There's also gift stuff—posters, cards, magazines—and a small gallery that shows homoerotic exhibitions.

Tattooing and body piercing... Though there are dozens of tattoo shops in the city, finding one with night-time hours can be a taxing chore. During the summertime **Hanky Panky** (tel 020/627–4848; Oudezijds Voorburg-wal 141; tram 4, 9, 16, 20, 24, or 25) keeps its needles working until 10pm, but in the colder months the doors shut by 6. A 16-year mainstay on the tattoo front, Hanky Panky is a high-profile parlor where visiting rock stars stop in to add to their epidermal collection. **Louise's Tattoo Parlor** (tel 020/638–0868; Palmdwarsstraat 15; tram 3; by appointment) is the city's only women-run tattoo parlor, though its clientele includes both sexes and all persua-sions. The small, hygenic shop officially closes at 6pm, but late-night appointments will be accommodated if you phone ahead. For piercing, branding, and scarification, **Body Manipulations** has two shops (tel 020/623–1937; Stromarkt 11; tram 4, 9, 16, 20, 24, or 25 and tel 020/638–4639; Oude Hoogstraat 31; tram 4, 9, 16, 24, or 25; Metro Nieuwmarkt; both shops open Thur until 9) run by English-speaking staffs who also serve as models for the shop's handiwork. A detailed English Q&A sheet covers the bases for the curious, and the color photos decorating the shop astound—check out the one with the man hoist-ing a concrete block with chains that pierce his nipples.

Now and zen... The New Age movement has found fertile ground in Holland, where a history of tolerance, religious freedom, and nonjudgmental expcrimentation has flour-ished for years. To get your chakras aligned and give your mantra a workout, try **De Roos** (tel 020/689–0081; Vondelstraat 35–37; tram 1, 2, 3, 5, 6, 11, or 12; open Mon–Sat until 11pm, Sun until 9:30), a New Age mini-mall with a bookshop, tea garden, and a center sponsoring classes in zen meditation, yoga, healing, and tarot card reading. A closet-sized and incense-scented room called Het Ving is the official info center; it's papered with brochures, leaflets, booklets, and newspapers. **Oibibio**

HANGING OUT ꙮ THE LOWDOWN

(see "Views from above," above) looks airlifted from California. Rough-hewn wood on the walls, Enya on the tape deck, and designer natural stuff like the Aveda line, hand-carved wooden kids toys, and environmentally correct everything. It's slicker than De Roos and a bit pricier. To keep that New Age feeling coming—and scope out last-minute, bliss-inducing souvenirs—head for **Erica** (tel 020/626–1842; in the middle tunnel of Centraal Station; all trams to Centraal Station, Metro Centraal Station; open Mon–Sat until 8), one of a Netherlands chain of New Age drugstores with shelves of homeopathic salves, remedies, and potions, essential oils, cruelty-free cosmetics, vitamins, health foods, and anything that can be harmoniously applied to the body.

Seminars... New Agers haven't cornered the market on evening classes. **Vrouwenhuis**—the name means "women house"—(tel 020/625–2066; Nieuwe Herengracht 95; open Mon–Thur until 11pm) celebrates the sisterhood kicked into gear by Betty Friedan, Germaine Greer, et al., and hosts self-defense classes, cultural events, a chess club, art exhibits, and an array of women-oriented activities. Drop-ins are welcome. If none of the classes suits you, pony up to the bar, where a cozy social scene is at work nightly. Of the same stripe, **Avalon** (tel 020/664–6530; Roerstraat 79; open nightly until 10, closed Sun) bills itself as a feminist spirituality center that offers XX-chromosome workshops, courses, and seminars. For cross-gender enrichment, **Universal Seminars** (tel 020/622–9742 or write for info: Leidsestraat 106ii, 1017 PG Amsterdam) is on the cusp of the city's New Age movement and sponsors workshops and seminars on personal growth and other warm, fuzzy topics. Because the speakers come from around the world, many of the evening lectures are in English.

Walk the walk... Meandering aimlessly is when serendipity is more apt to unfold, and nighttime walking in Amsterdam is safe and beguiling. For a bit of history, context, and commentary, the VVV's 90-minute **Street-walking tour** (reserve in person at one of the VVV's offices: inside Centraal Station, opposite the Centraal Station, on the Leidseplein, on the Stadionplein; tours at 8pm, Thur–Sun, April 1–Sept 30; Dfl 25) is led by a guide, usually a university student, who takes small groups through *de Walletjes* (the Red Light District), the oldest section of town, where the world's oldest profession is openly professed. The area is rich in city (and titty) history and tours wend by churches, picturesque waterfront houses, and conclude with a visit to the PG-rated Erotic Museum (you've probably seen nastier things on the bottom of your shoe). For a wider pedestrian scope of the city, the VVV also sponsors evening walks through **Jordaan** and **the city center** (reserve in person at VVV offices; 8:30pm, Sat, Sun, and Wed; 2 hours; Dfl 24.50). For the city center walk, guides shepherd small groups through the Red Light District, past squares and monuments, historical points of interest (Look, Marge, it's the city's oldest wooden house!!) and end at a cafe for a chummy glass of beer.

Don't be afraid to hoof it on your own if you're struck down by an unforeseen burst of Greta Garbo Syndrome— even though it may be difficult to cure in Amsterdam (pop. 800,000) without holing up in your hotel room and assiduously pondering your navel. But, seriously, it can be done. It is best to *meamble*—reverentially wander—the city, remembering that tours provide a framework while true exploration is an individual enterprise. Pull a Robert Frost and take the road less traveled, which means getting outside the *grachtengordel* (literally, golden girdle, the ring of canals that gives the city center its horseshoe shape). The area west of Amsterdam's city center, **Scheepvaarts-buurt** is one of the less trafficked sections. Haarlemmerstraat and Haarlemmerdijk are the main streets of this funky neighborhood, which resembles New York City's Soho or Paris' Marais before gentrification took over and rents went up. Lining the streets are warehouses, boutiques, artists' spaces, makeshift galleries, and restaurants usually frequented by people in the 'hood. At the far end of the Haarlemmerdijk, benches face the water and a rangy flotilla of houseboats. Chances are you'll be uninterrupted for long stretches of time.

late nigh

6

t dining

Pancakes crowned with gloppy dressings? Meat and potatoes? No thanks. Going Dutch in Amsterdam means skipping Dutch food. The locals are hip to the generally unappetizing nature of their carbo-loaded repasts. They also don't call splitting the tab with your date "Going Dutch." Amsterdammers may be a shade too casual to take gender roles seriously, but the phrase is out-of-date. When Amsterdammers suggest a Dutch meal, they'll probably steer you toward an Indonesian restaurant and mutter something about Indonesia being a former colony so it sort of counts as traditional food, right? If the Richter scale of spiciness registers too high for Indonesian, global cuisine has admirable representation here, especially food from the Pacific Rim, which is all the rage on the local food front.

Among the stereotypes of European culture that the Dutch shatter is the notion of dining late at night. Typically, the city's denizens are at the dinner table—either at home or in a restaurant—between 7 and 8pm. For the traveler, this presents two scenarios: occasional difficulty securing a table in a restaurant frequented by locals if you saunter in after 8:30, and a dearth of restaurants open after midnight. Restaurants here are smaller, which means fewer tables (and a surfeit of the warm 'n' fuzzy *gezzeligheid* endemic in the city); yet reservations are not the norm. Hurrying diners and turning tables are alien notions. Late night dining (and people-watching and style-mongering and pre-club or post-theater noshing) means eating in one of the city's 1,500 cafes. Amsterdam surpasses Paris in the exuberant way it embraces its cafe culture. Cafes are mess halls, rest stops, sidewalk theaters, fueling stations— the nexus of the city's social life. Differentiated from restaurants by their abbreviated menus, they usually feature some variety of highbrow pub grub: salads, soups, pastas, sandwiches. Cafes are open until 2 or 3am serving beer, coffee, and food. For food in the wee hours, only a handful of bona fide restaurants are still cooking—Bojo, an Indonesian place where patrons are likely to be chemically altered and outlandishly attired clubgoers, and Thijm Nachtcafé, favored by the young, the mod, the pierced, the bloodshot. For a quick fix, the only recourses are Febos (automatlike stores with greasy selections awaiting behind tiny silver doors), pizza-by-the-slice joints on the Damrak, or overlit falafel places on Leidseplein with unappetizingly blurry food shots in the storefront window.

Late Night Dining in the Museumplein Area & Amsterdam South

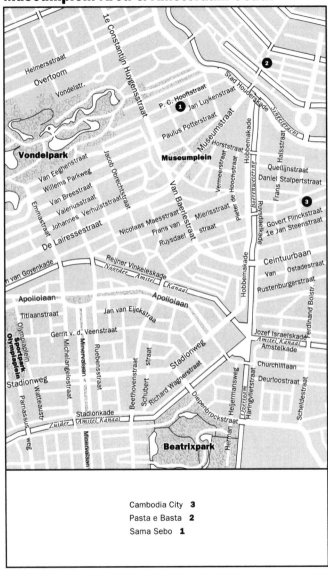

Cambodia City **3**

Pasta e Basta **2**

Sama Sebo **1**

Central Amsterdam Late Night Dining

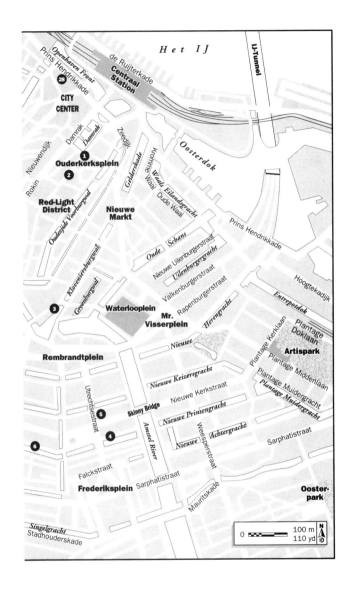

The Lowdown

Greek... Owner Mike Karantzounis (a Greco-Dutch Don Ho) welcomes diners behind the gold velvet curtain into **Plaka,** a chummy, candlelit restaurant in the Soho-like streets of Jordaan. Multilanguage menus ease navigation through the typical Greek selections; combo platters help satisfy the vacationer's impulse to sample everything in sight. The food is fresh and surprisingly light on the grease factor, and the portions run large. A pair of appetizers makes a full meal, and the vegetarian plate can easily sate two. By meal's end, Mike gets heavy-handed with the complimentary Metaxa. Patrons hoist snifters of the firewater and laugh their way through toasts. On bawdier nights, Mike leads diners in tabletop dancing. Opa! As clean as a hospital lab, **Grekas Traiterie**'s white-tiled interior gleams like an advertisement for Mr. Clean. Behind a glass counter, silver vats of fresh Greek dishes taunt: dolmades, spanikopita, moussaka, tsaziki, treacly trays of baklava. Tucked between a spate of antiquarian bookstores and three-star hotels, Grekas is mostly used as a takeout restaurant by locals, but six tables accommodate guests who are bent on immediate gratification (or who don't want to eat their gyros back in the hotel room).

Italian... There are fewer than a dozen tables squeezed into tiny **Hostaria,** so be careful not to splash the house red on your neighbor's white linen dress when you refill your glass. Owners Massimo and Marjolein Pasquinoli imbue this Jordaan restaurant with garlic, warmth, jocularity, fresh bread, classic Italian food, and a no-rush attitude that says linger over your carpaccio, your insalata, your espresso, your cannoli. Dancing at **Pasta e Basta** is performance gastronomy of the most haute variety. Opera singers with creamy voices serenade patrons while they select from glistening platters of antipasti arrayed on the top of a 19th-century grand piano. This is one of the few restaurants in town with a dress code, though it's fashion by osmosis: there's no written management request for little black designer dresses and sports coats, but that's what you'll see. You'll notice that for the most part patrons twirl their main-course pasta rather nonchalantly if not absent-mindedly—what they're really doing is scanning the room for high-octane guests. In a city as relentlessly casual as Amsterdam, these traces of the New York and Paris see-and-be-seen scene seem a bit out of kilter, but the local nouveaux riches do need someplace to pose.

Vegetarian... The dewy waitresses at **De Bolhoed** have a faint air of Peggy Lipton of "Mod Squad" fame. They scuttle between tables and chairs that look like hand-painted refugees from flea markets, serving ample plates of vegetarian and vegan dishes from a daily changing menu. Keith Jarrett music tinkles in the background; art magazines lie on tabletops next to sea salt and pepper. When it's warm, a handful of tables are dragged outside next to Prinsengracht for people-watching. Amsterdam is dotted with Japanese restaurants serving astonishingly overpriced, compact food that leaves you profoundly hungry an hour later. **Shizen**, though, earns marks as one of the best for authentic atmosphere, macrobiotic meals, and affordable sushi. (The average tab runs about Dfl 35 for sushi, an appetizer, and a warm flacon of sake.) Half of the dining room has Western-style tables and chairs, the other offers shoeless tatami-mat seating. The fish and vegetable offerings are fresh and plentiful and they fortunately avoid the self-important austerity macrobiotic food is often prone to.

Indonesian... The hearty appeal of traditional Dutch meat-and-potatoes meals notwithstanding, for a truly exotic, convivial, and flavorful meal you'll have to go to an Indonesian restaurant. The fiery, rice-based cuisine of the former colony has been dazzling Dutch diners ever since it was introduced to the motherland, and Indonesian restaurants have multiplied over the years. The most traditional type of Indonesian meal is the *rijsttafel*, a spicy smorgasbord of mounds of rice and 20 or so bowls of spiced meats, fish, and vegetables lined up on warming

LATE NIGHT DINING ⏽ THE LOWDOWN

trays. It's generally smart to first have a conversation with your waiter about flammability. Though most Indonesian places tone down the spiciness so as not to kill off a fair percentage of the population, the zing factor can be overwhelming if left unchecked. That said, however, it's the cook's propensity to pump up the volume on the curries and peppers that lure adventurous diners to **Tempo Doeloe** on quietly stylish Utrechtsestraat. If *Wayne's World* did restaurant reviews, they'd call this place House of Burning Tongue. Wayne himself, though, would probably feel out of place in the well-worn opulence of Doeloe's dining room: candelabras, linen tablecloths, Victorian vases streaming with flowers, frilly chandeliers, and pink wall paneling provide a surprisingly genteel setting for the chef's culinary pyrotechnics. If the place is full (as it often is), duck toward the four-seater back bar framed by business cards, nurse a beer, and ask the bartender to point out Yoko Ono's AmEx bill. Photos of Indonesia hang from walls covered with bamboo mats and ceiling fans provide a gentle breeze at *Speciaal*, a deservedly popular restaurant in Jordaan. Ask for a table with Raymond, a waiter who's been on board for 10 years. He'll recommend *rijsttafel*, Grolsch on tap, and *spekkoek*, a brown-and-white-striped pound cake made of pumpkin and cinnamon. In the midst of all the Gold Card real estate on P.C. Hooftstraat, the city's version of Rodeo Drive, is **Sama Sebo.** The draw here is the cluster of outdoor tables for summertime eating and people-watching. The menu covers the basic Indonesian classics—*rijsttafel*, *gado gado* (meat with peanut sauce), satay, and rice and noodle dishes—plus the chef will make any dish meatless for you.

Elegance is everything... Hand-holding and smoldering looks aren't on the menu, but they seem to accompany each course at **Restaurant Blanko**, a basement-level cubbyhole of a restaurant on Prinsengracht. Classical music wafts through the air. Officious waiters flutter around the half dozen tables, serving Continental standbys to a moneyed and well-heeled crowd, most of whom are fueling up for an evening of ballet or theater. Anchoring a corner of Leidseplein, one of the city's busiest squares, is the landmark **Café Americain.** Wily Mata Hari hosted her wedding reception here amid the splendor and elegant eye candy of its art deco and art nouveau interior. The food is French lite, but the menu is secondary. The real meal is the Dutch *Jugendstijl* architecture, the circa-1920 chandeliers, leaded glass windows, velvet-upholstered chairs, and the spirits of the writers and artists who have gathered here since 1897. **Oibibio** is one of the city's grander "grand cafes," a term used to denote high-ceilinged, sophisticated establishments peopled primarily by an intensely urban, under-50 crowd. A mirrored bar anchors one end of the airy main dining room; at the other end two levels of seating are suffused with light from floor-to-ceiling windows. There's a separate restaurant on the second floor as well as a Japanese tea garden. The same menu of inventive vegetarian creations is available in all three dining areas.

Asian... The cuisines of the Pacific Rim are well represented here. **Cambodia City** doesn't rack up any points for interior design. It's unmistakably a neighborhood joint, something the Dutch call an *eethuis* (eat house). What it does have going for it are the large portions, savvy local clientele, and a prime location on Albert Cuypstraat, site of the city's daily carnival-*cum*-flea market. The servings of soup could feed small villages (the crab soup is particularly tasty). Those suffering from menu paralysis can opt for sampler platters. **Singha**, one of the city's newest Thai restaurants, is tucked into a shady residential side street off of Utrechtsestraat. The service can be a bit leisurely, but the atmospherics—candlelight, walls awash in muted pastels, the sound of the sizzling wok in the kitchen—lull the senses while you wait. Gerard, the owner, translates the menu and invariably recommends the Thai beer that bears the name of his restaurant.

Mexican... Step into **Pacifico**, a boisterous Mexican restaurant on the fringes of the Red Light District, and you'll find yourself wondering how the Dutch managed to transplant a piece of the *pais* across the Atlantic. A narrow space, whitewashed walls, worn stone floors, woodbeamed ceilings, artistically chipped paint—*and* chefs who don't drown meals in cheese. Tuesday's margarita night (Dfl 5 for a small glass) is a good time to drop in; the patrons tend to linger and grow more friendly. **Rose's Cantina** is *not* the place to go if you want to write in your journal, propose marriage, or reveal long-hidden secrets to an old friend. It's boisterous, crowded, loud, and busy, busy, busy. The burritos, tacos, enchiladas, and tortillas are all standard issue (steer clear of the gummy guacamole), but the margaritas will make you feel invincible. For the most authentic Mexican food in town, duck into **Burrito** near Vondelpark and try to ignore the fact that the place is run by an Egyptian. Order the restaurant's namesake engorged with chicken, pork, or tangy beans. The menu also includes a healthy selection of veggie dishes.

French... Jean Jean is the living-room-sized restaurant that Jordaan locals favor for French food because it serves very fine regional specialties *sans* the attitude that often accompanies Franco cuisine. Though the cooking here is worthy of fancier digs, the dress code is Gap casual and the decor is minimal, to say the least. (They definitely didn't hire an interior designer.) The waiters don't shoo you from the table as you linger over your four-course prix fixe meal; nor do they roll their eyes when you click your Kodak to preserve that moment when the flaming ladle of Grand Marnier cascades onto the crêpes suzette. To increase your chances of getting a table, arrive between 7 and 8 (locals eat early and linger, a most civilized approach). Wear something Italian and black if you want to look like the natives who dine at **Le Zinc... et Les Dames**, an achingly chic, bilevel French restaurant in a converted warehouse on Prinsengracht. A selection of ten wines accompanies a daily three-course menu of regional specialties such as *saucisson de Lyon*, mussel salad with seaweed, and *tarte tatin*. The zinc bar on the ground floor serves red wine by the glass to a nonchalantly savvy crowd of business and media types and assorted bonbon babes.

Budget... Sophisticated Dutch chefs might turn up their noses at the suggestion that they add *pannekoeken* (pancakes) to their menus. These graceless crêpes may be as traditional as wooden shoes, but a culinary triumph they're not. Nevertheless, just as a trip to the South means eating grits, a trip to Amsterdam isn't complete if you haven't had a *pannekoek* or two. You may be used to thinking of pancakes as breakfast food, but in the

Netherlands, they come in lunch, dinner, and dessert varieties. The entrée pancakes come with all sorts of meat and vegetable "stuffings"; served for dessert, they're often covered with a fruit syrup called *stroop*. Go ahead, order a dozen: this Dutch comfort food makes for a benign, rib-sticking meal, something your gastrointestinal system might need after too many nights of fiery Indonesian fare. The **Pancake Bakery**, in the basement of a converted Prinsengracht warehouse, lists 70 combo fillings, including the "American" with corn, fried chicken, carrots, and Cajun sauce—it's as yucky as it sounds, but if you're feeling homesick…. Popular with students and faculty from the nearby University of Amsterdam, **Café Het Palais** has the earnest casualness (and the large-portion/low-price axiom) of a college cafe. Salads, sandwiches, pasta dishes, and soups round out the menu. The sidewalk tables—coveted during fine weather—are filled with people reading, jostling notebooks, or deconstructing life, art, and beauty through clouds of cigarette smoke. "Half price plus one guilder" promises **Rimini's** advertisement for its pizza and pasta dishes. Open until midnight, the wattage from the fluorescent lights may steer away those more interested in atmosphere than economic austerity, but the tab for a 14-inch pizza and a couple of beers rings in at less than Dfl 10. The trailer-park-esque crowd runs toward those in need of dental work, a fashion makeover, or sobriety. Things get hairy from 11pm until closing time.

After midnight… Restaurant choices narrow drastically for those interested in eating after the witching hour. Most restaurants close or stop serving meals at 11pm. Though cafes have small menus of dishes that aren't too extravagant or country-specific (cheese plates, salads, pastas, cuts of beef, sandwiches, and soups), the Dutch often gather there just to drink and people-watch. But for those who might want to dine after a night of culture, here's the scoop. At **Bojo**, there's much good news: The kitchen cooks Indonesian food until 2am. The food's tasty and plentiful, and it has all the necessary properties to absorb the alcohol and THC that might be skating through your bloodstream. The bad news is that the restaurant is on a tacky, honky-tonk street packed with bars, clubs, and tourists. Since this is the city's only sit-down restaurant open after-hours, it draws the seamiest mix of Amsterdam's post-club yahoos. Count on sharing your meal with a roomful of belligerent, tattooed drunks and very spaced-out critters on God-knows-what. Don't be surprised if the couple at the next table suddenly engages in what was known in high school as heavy petting. Crowds are generally tamer at **Café Thijssen**, a neo-brown cafe ("neo" only because the walls haven't yet darkened from a zillion years of accumulated cigarette smoke). Opened by three friends who were area barflies, Thijssen is a neighborhood joint that went to finishing school. Just across from the visually stunning canal, Brouwersgracht, Thijssen's indoor and sidewalk tables are busy but not choked. *Broodjes* (soups), cheese platters, and salads are served until 1am. As the name suggests, **Thijm Nachtcafé and Restaurant** serves food in the post-midnight realm; until 3:30am the kitchen cranks out wholesome dishes that cover most of the food groups. For a nosh instead of a feed, you'll find overlit, pizza-by-the-slice joints on Damrak, in the Red Light District, and on Leidseplein. Falafel and *showarma* places are as ubiquitous as McDonald's in the States, but most people find the high lard factor makes much of the food inedible. The urge for refined sugar in all its seductive incarnations brings clubgoers to **Gary's Late Nite**, a little shop that serves bagels, chocolate-chip cookies, and muffins to the party creatures who troll the night partaking in depressants of the licit and illicit varieties.

Where the arty eat... For incomparable people-watching, try to snag one of the sidewalk tables at glittery **Cafe Luxembourg**, an ab-fab, see-and-be-seen hangout frequented by yuppies and their sycophants. The cafe food is an afterthought. The crowd is the meal. Chew the buzz. If you do want to eat, expect an abbreviated cafe menu, with a few pastas, ratatouille, and the like. The cooking is more than competent, but people come here primarily to drink coffee and while away time. **Cafe de Jaren** has visible cachet. Reminiscent of a casually hip restaurant in New York's SoHo, the two-story waterside cafe is a soaring, spiffed-up warehouse full of University of Amsterdam grad students—they like to park themselves at the center reading table and flip through art magazines. You can count the tourist boats on the

Amstel from the bilevel outdoor terraces while you select a soup or pasta from an abbreviated menu. Out on the western fringes of the city, **Café West Pacific** shares a charmingly grimy piece of a former gas factory, the Westergasfabriek, with an exhibition hall, dance club, party hall, and experimental performance arts venue. This is definitely Kerouac territory—cigarette smoking and palpable angst are mandatory. The menu changes weekly, but the appetizers remain (the steamed artichoke smothered with goat cheese and olives is pretty close to a sexual experience). Though it's the canalside terrace out back that is the prime real estate, the interior of **SAS** looks like a college art studio after class. Unframed canvases and found-object assemblages clutter the space; there are mismatched tables and chairs painted in bright colors. Want a candelabrum made out of old typewriters? Ask. It might be for sale. Candlelight illuminates the faces of the carelessly stylish patrons. Guitar and harmonica players provide occasional live background music. The menu includes quiche, lasagna, and a couple of decent cuts of beef.

For takeout... At the Thai restaurant **Singha**, all 47 items on the menu are available for takeout until the 11:30pm closing time. Either phone in or sit yourself down and nurse a beer while the kitchen slices, dices, and spices. How do you say "couch potato" in Dutch? For those nights when you're just too wiped out to hit the town, the prescription could be good, old Chinese takeout. **Kam Yin**, just steps from Centraal Station, lovingly cradles the takeout standards—lo mein, egg rolls, and such—in Styrofoam containers. The restaurant is an MSG-free zone, but also tends to go light on seasonings. Request extra soy sauce.

The Index

$$$	Dfl 40 and above	$26 and above
$$	Dfl 20–Dfl 40	$28–$26
$	Under Dfl 20	under $18

Major credit cards (American Express, MasterCard, Visa) are accepted where noted.

Bojo. One of the few Amsterdam restaurants serving food past midnight. The cheap, plentiful Indonesian meals are a boon for granola-heads, clubgoers, and night owls with a predilection for big grub and street theater.... *Tel 020/ 622–7434. Lange Leidsedwarsstraat 51; tram 1, 2, 5, 6, 7, 10, or 11. Open Mon–Thur until 2am, Fri and Sat until 3. $$*

De Bolhoed. New Agers, hippies, vegetarians, and the planet's other mellow subgroups converge at this funky Jordaan restaurant for fresh, daily changing vegan and vegetarian dishes. Outside tables.... *Tel 020/626–1803. Prinsengracht 60-62; tram 10, 13, 14, or 17. Open daily until 10pm. $*

Burrito. Satisfyingly spicy Mexican staples-enchiladas, tacos, and such-in a cozy cafe on the fringes of the city center.... *Tel 020/618–9807. De Clerqstraat 14; tram 10, 13, 14, or 17. Open daily until 11pm. MC accepted. $*

Café Americain. The place where Mata Hari once hosted her wedding reception is now a popular cafe with a resplendent art deco interior and a crowded sidewalk terrace.... *Tel 020/623–4813. American Hotel, Leidseplein 28; tram 1, 2, 5, 6, 7, 10, or 11. Open daily until midnight. Major credit cards accepted. $$*

Café Het Palais. A comfy student hangout with a sunny terrace and a kitchen commandoed by a couple of Aussies who cook hearty, Yankee-ish meals (heavy on the stews, soups, salads) for budget prices.... *Tel 020/626–0600. Paleisstraat 16; tram 1, 2, or 5. Open Mon–Thur until 1am, Fri and Sat until 2. $*

Cafe de Jaren. Grand cafe on the Amstel with airy interior swathed in tile and abstract paintings. In summer the bilevel outdoor terraces hum with a good-looking cross-section of hipsters, travelers, and literati. Cafe food downstairs includes ample tureens of soup, pasta dishes, and salads.... *Tel 020/625–5771. Nieuwe Doelenstraat 20; tram 4, 9, 14, 16, 24, or 25. Restaurant serves until 11pm, cafe until 1am. $$*

Cafe Luxembourg. Top-rate, snacky, cafe food includes dim sum, crab sandwiches, and pasta with porcini mushrooms. Stellar people-watching, especially at the sidewalk tables.... *Tel 020/620–6264. Spuistraat 22–24; tram 1, 2, 5, 11, 13, or 17. Open Mon–Thur and Sun until 1am, Fri and Sat until 2. $$*

Café Thijssen. A Jordaan neo-brown cafe with a lot of camaraderie and a circle of regulars that rivals the cast of "Cheers." Standard pub grub; the atmosphere and people-watching are the draws.... *Tel 020/623–8994. Brouwersgracht 107; bus 18 or 22. Open daily until 2am. $–$$*

Café West Pacific. Housed in Westergasfabriek, a former gas factory, this space also accommodates performances, exhibitions, a dance floor, and a cafe with about 10 selections tilted toward veggie dishes with tangy sauces.... *Tel 020/597–4458. Haarlemmerweg 8-10; tram 10. Open Tue–Sun until 1am, Fri and Sat until 2; food served until 11pm. $$*

Cambodia City. Hole-in-the-wall restaurant with zilch decor and budget-priced Vietnamese and Thai food just off one of the city's liveliest street markets.... *Tel 020/671-4930. Albert Cuypstraat 58–60; tram 16, 24, or 25. Open daily until 10pm. $*

LATE NIGHT DINING 〰 THE INDEX

Gary's Late Nite. A stop-and-nosh place in the midst of a club-clotted street. Cookies, bagels, muffins, and other treats heavy on refined sugar.... *Tel 020/420–2406. Reguliersdwarsstraat 53; tram 1, 2, 5, or 11. Open Sun– Thur until 3am, Fri and Sat until 4. $*

Grekas Traiterie. Spic-and-span Greek takeout joint with a half dozen tables just in case the aroma of spanikopita, dol- mades, and baklava overwhelms you on the spot.... *Tel 020/620–3590. Singel 131; tram 1, 2, 5, or 11. Open Tue–Sun until 11pm. $–$$*

Hostaria. Low lighting, high decibels, hearty laughter, the aroma of garlic and onions, jugs of outstanding house red—you'll find all this along with excellent Italian food in this Jordaan neighborhood restaurant.... *Tel 020/626– 0028. 2e Egelantiersdwarsstraat 9; tram 10, 13, 14, or 17. Open daily until 11:30pm. Major credit cards accepted. $$*

Jean Jean. Outstanding French food in an unpretentious Jordaan restaurant. Three prix fixe menus, escargots with potent powers, and superior crêpes suzette.... *Tel 020/ 627–7153. Eerste Anjeliersdwarsstraat 12–14; tram 10, 13, 14, or 17. Open daily until midnight. Reservations rec- ommended on weekends. $$–$$$*

Kam Yin. Huge and budget-priced portions of Surinamese and Chinese noodle dishes, just two minutes from Centraal Station.... *Tel 020/625–3115. Warmoesstraat 6; tram 4, 9, 14, 16, 20, 24, or 25. Open daily until midnight. Takeout available. $*

Oibibio. An airy, architecturally stunning grand cafe connected to a New Age center with bookstore, Japanese tea garden, boutique, and sauna. Enya territory.... *Tel 020/553–9355. Prins Hendrikkade 20–21; tram 1, 2, 4, 5, 9, 11, 13, 17, 24, or 25; Metro Centraal Station. Open Mon-Thur and Sun until 1am; Fri, Sat until 2am. Major credit cards accepted. $$*

Pacifico. Gregarious crowds, Tex-Mex food, and tiny yet delec- table margaritas in a small bodega just outside of the Red

Light District.... *Tel 020/624–2911. Warmoesstraat 31; tram 4, 9, 14, 16, 20, 24, or 25. Open daily until 11pm. Major credit cards accepted.* $$–$$$

The Pancake Bakery. When in Rome... typical (and cheap) Dutch fare in a basement-level restaurant. Choose from more than five dozen fillings.... *Tel 020/625–1333. Prinsengracht 191; tram 13, 14, or 17. Open daily until 11pm.* $$

Pasta e Basta. Highbrow and high-culture pasta restaurant with chichi clientele and serenading opera singers. Reservations a must; the wait can stretch up to two weeks.... *Tel 020/ 422–2226. Nieuwe Spiegelstraat 8. Open daily until 11pm. Major credit cards accepted.* $$$

Plaka. Owner Mike Karantzounis presides over a kitchen serving fresh Greek dishes in a candlelit Jordaan restaurant adorned with Hellenic kitsch.... *Tel 020/627–9338. Egelantiersstraat 124; tram 13, 14, or 17. Open Mon-Sat until midnight.* $$

Restaurant Blanko. Classical music, linen, and Continental fare in a clubby basement-level dining room that encourages hand-holding.... *Tel 020/625–9232. Prinsengracht 512 sous; tram 13, 14, or 17. Open only Thur, Fri, and Sat 6–11:30pm; closed otherwise. Major credit cards accepted. Reservations recommended.* $$$

Rimini. Cheapo pizza place good for solid Italian carbo-loading. A meal and a beer cost less than Dfl 10.... *Tel 020/622– 7014. Lange Leidsedwarsstraat 75. Open daily until midnight.* $

Rose's Cantina. It's a jungle in there—popular, raucous, aromatic, and fun. Powerful margaritas and standard Mexican staples.... *Tel 020/625–9797. Reguliersdwarsstraat 38; tram 1, 2, 5, 11, 16, 24, or 25. Open daily until 11:30pm. Major credit cards accepted.* $–$$

Sama Sebo. The sidewalk tables at this well-known Indonesian restaurant on one of Amsterdam's toniest shopping streets make it possible for guests to engage in some world-class people-watching while they sample the 20-dish *rijsttafel.... Tel 020/662–8146. P. C. Hooftstraat 27; tram 2, 3, 5, or 12. Open Mon–Sat until midnight. Major credit cards accepted. Reservations recommended. $$–$$$*

SAS. It's like eating in a 1920s drawing room. Worn sofas and armchairs interspersed with dining tables. Candlelight warms the eclectic montage of wall art and artifacts. Soups, salads, pasta dishes are served on the canalside terrace out back.... *Tel 020/420–4075. Marnixstraat 79; tram 7, 10, or 17. Open Mon–Thur until 1am, Fri and Sat until 2. $–$$*

Shizen. Tatami-mat seating, reasonable prices, and a vegetarian menu in a hushed little Japanese oasis off a zoo of a street. Tasty sashimi; delicious *ebi kushi yaki* (grilled shrimp on a skewer with teriyaki sauce).... *Tel 020/622–8672. Kerkstraat 148; tram 1, 2, or 5. Open Mon–Sat until 11pm. Major credit cards accepted. $$*

Singha. Awash in pastels, lit with candles, and tucked into an achingly picturesque side street, this Thai restaurant lists more than four dozen dishes on its menu.... *Tel 020/625–4189. Utrechtsedwarsstraat 107; tram 4, 6, 7, and 10. Open daily until 10:30pm. Major credit cards accepted. Takeout available. $$–$$$*

Speciaal. The 20-dish *rijsttafel* packs them in night after night at this small Indonesian restaurant in Jordaan.... *Tel 020/624–9706. Nieuwe Leliestraat 142; tram 10, 13, or 14. Open daily until midnight. Major credit cards accepted. Reservations recommended on Fri and Sat. $$*

Tempo Doeloe. The spiciest Indonesian food in Amsterdam served by light of candle and chandelier.... *Tel 020/625–6718. Utrechtsestraat 75; tram 4, 6, 7, or 10. Open daily until 11:30pm. Major credit cards accepted. Reservations recommended on Fri and Sat. $$–$$$*

Thijm Nachtcafé and Restaurant. One of a handful of post-midnight restaurants with a 2 to 3am rush hour for carbo-loading: pastas, rice dishes, sandwiches. Portions are hefty, prices border on budget…. *Tel 020/622–4541. Nieuwezijds Voorburgwal 163–165; tram 1, 2, 5, or 11. Open Wed–Sat until 5am; kitchen closes at 3:30am. $*

Le Zinc… et Les Dames. This warmly charming French cafe in a rustic canalside warehouse offers regional cooking in three-course tableaux. *Très romantic…. Tel 020/622–9044. Prinsengracht 999, tram 4. Open Tue–Sat until 11pm. Closed Mon–Tue. MC accepted. $$–$$$*

down
and
dirty

All-night pharmacies... The city's pharmacies take turns with late hours. Phone **Centrale Dokters Kienst** (tel 063/ 503–2042) for the one closest you. A multilingual staff answers the phone 24 hours a day.

Babysitters... The VVV gives its seal of approval to a trio of babysitters' organizations: **Oppascentrale Kriterion** (tel 020/624–5848); **Babysit Centrale UVV** (tel 020/662– 3650); and **De Oppaslijn** (tel 063/203–5032). Each organization will send a sitter to your hotel.

Emergencies... The 24-hour phone number for fire, police, and ambulance is **06–11**; no money is required for the call. The non-emergency central police number is **020/559– 9111**. Police stations are at: Lijnbaansgracht 219, Singel 455, Van Leijenberghlaan 15, Warmoesstraat 44, Nieuwezijds Voorburgwal, and Prinsengracht 1109.

Events information... It's difficult *not* to know what's going on in Amsterdam. The city is one big events hotline: Posters plaster the sides of buildings. Leaflets and brochures paper bars, restaurants, clubs, and cafes. Info will be heartily dispensed by bartenders, bouncers, the people at the adjoining table in the cafe where you're nursing a cappuccino or a lager. The **AUB** (Amsterdam Uitboro), or **Uitboro**, as it's also known (tel 020/621–1211 or 020/626–8811; Leidseplein 26; 10–6 Mon–Sat, 9–9 Thur), is a government-funded, cultural clearinghouse lined with leaflets, pamphlets, brochures, flyers, and any other variation of the printed notice about arts and cultural events in Amsterdam. It's also a one-stop entertainment ticketing agency and information office for music, dance, theater, and special events. The office also publishes *Culture in Amsterdam*, a two-year listing of all the city's big-time performances. For the "Sprockets" crowd there's *Concertagenda*, a newsletter published every other month by the mercilessly contemporary De IJsbreker Musiekcentrum; the program includes a concert calendar in English. Published biweekly by the VVV, *What's On In Amsterdam*, available at newsstands, larger hotels, and VVV offices (Dfl 3.50), lists the cultural events in the obvious venues. *Uitkrant* is a free monthly publication of theater, concert, and dance listings published by the AUB. Though it's written in Dutch, events are listed under venues, which makes it easy to decipher. You can pick it up at the AUB office (Leidseplein 26) and in clubs, coffeeshops, and bars around the city. *Luna* is a free monthly tabloid aimed at hipsters and younger culture vultures. The stories about nightlife in Amsterdam and Haarlem are indecipherable unless you speak Dutch, but the ads are funky and the club listings include some squat parties and roaming raves. Nightcrawlers and party monsters cling to *To The Point*, a colorful glossy sheet in English published twice a month; available in music stores, clubs, coffeeshops, bars, and cafes, it is considered the up-to-the-minute source of club info. *Gouden Gids,* the Dutch version of the Yellow Pages, publishes a free *Visitor's Guide* that's very comprehensive and includes listings for doctors, dentists, and fax centers. For the mellow traveler and the more organically inclined, *Amsterdam Connection Magazine*, a free quarterly half English/half Dutch, gives details about New Age-y restaurants, bookstores, accommodations, centers, and markets.

Festivals and special events...

January: **Oudejaarsavond** is the Dutch term for New Year's Eve and the celebration here transpires much as it does in other cosmopolitan cities worldwide—fireworks, public drunkenness, spontaneous kissing, cheering, mirth, retrospection, resolution, champagne. Restaurants, bars, and cafes remain open late in the evening (and the morning).

February: On the 25th, Amsterdammers commemorate the **1941 Dockworkers' Strike**, which occurred after 400 young Jewish men were arrested and shipped away to their execution because a Nazi had been killed during a street fight. The protest strike by dock and transport workers crippled the city. On the anniversary day, the Dokwerker Monument at J.D. Meijerplein is decorated with a wreath.

March: **Stille Omgang** (Silent Procession) may be the only holiday on record that commemorates vomiting. Celebrated on the Sunday closest to March 15, and marked with a silent nighttime procession through the city to Sint Nicholaaskerk, the procession honors the Miracle of Amsterdam, when in 1345 a dying man vomited the bread he was fed during his last rites. The discharge was thrown onto a fire and found unaltered the next morning among the ashes; the man recovered and a miracle was decreed. (Contact Gezelschap van de Stille Omgang, tel 023–345415, Sandvoortseweg 59). During the third week of March, the Meervaart Theater's **Blues Festival** brings international blues acts to town.

April: It's tulip time, the unofficial segue from spring to summer, and the month is kicked off by the **Stadsilluminatie**, when the lights around the canal bridges are illuminated for the first time after the winter; they continue to twinkle every evening until October. During the last week, **Nationaal Museumweekend** means free entry to all museums in the Netherlands. **Koninginnedag** (Queen's Day) on Apr 30 is the blowout, citywide party of the year, with bits of Mardi Gras, Carnival, and New Year's Eve rolled into one. The festivities begin the night of the Apr 29 and last well into the early-morning hours of May 1. Bars and restaurants feature special menus and stay open later. Musicians roam the street and much revelry ensues. In addition to being a genuine bacchanal, Queen's Day is also a consumer holiday—streets and yards are dotted with makeshift stalls, forming a citywide flea market.

May: **Herdenkingsdag** (Remembrance Day) on May 4 and **Bevrijkingsdag** (Liberation Day) on May 5 are back-to-back government holidays involving speeches, a visit by the Queen, and a remembrance of the Dutch who died during WWII. **Oosterparkfestival**, a three-day street festival designed to celebrate the city's ethnicities, is held on the first weekend in May in Oosterpark. Throughout the month the **World Press Photo Exhibition** takes over the nave of the Nieuwe Kerk.

June: **The Holland Festival**, a highbrow nationwide festival of opera, theater, dance, and music, spreads its cultural performances through Amsterdam and other major Dutch cities. Runners clog city streets on the second Sunday of the month to participate in the **Canal Run** (Echo Grachtenloop); 3-, 6-, and 11-mile courses loop along the canals. The highlight of **Gay Pride Week**, the last week of the month, is the **Festival van Verleiding**, a weekend of performance art, drag shows, comedy, parties, and exhibitions at the popular club **Melkweg** (see The Arts).

July: **Rendezvous,** an annual 10-day AIDS fundraiser in mid-July, features dozens of local bands performing free outdoor concerts while volunteers canvas for donations for research.

August: During **Uitmarkt** (last weekend of the month), cultural organizations from around the Netherlands perform gratis indoors, and out, for three days to entice Amsterdammers to attend their concert, theater, opera, and dance programs in the upcoming season. For sports fans, the **Amsterdam 700**, during the first or second week, is when Ajax Amsterdam (the city's soccer team) meets other

European teams for a weekend of preseason competition. The **Prinsengrachtconcert**, one of the city's stateliest free events, is held the last week of the month. Musicians perform classical music on a boat on the Prinsengracht outside of the quietly stylish and moneyed Pulitzer Hotel (tel 020/626–8485).

September: **Jordaan Festival** (second and third weeks) on Elandsgracht includes street-food stalls, entertainment, themed parties in local bars, a fair with rides, and a cabaret in the Palm Building (no phone, Palmstraat 34). **Hiswa te Water** is a boat show at the Oosterdok. The visual highlight is a nighttime parade of canoes outlined with lights.

October: Though a meteorologist would disagree, the Dutch say it's winter when Leidseplein has frozen solid enough to be converted into an ice rink. This usually occurs by the second or third week.

November: During the first two weeks the **Stagedoor Theater Festival** (held at Baili, Engelenbak, and Soeterijn theaters) offers experimental theater and performances in the city center, while the **Over Het IJ Festival** offers the same on the northern side of town (north of the IJ). **Sinterklaas**, the Dutch Santa Claus parade (mid-November), is the harbinger of the Christmas season. Santa disembarks from a steamboat at Centraal Station, mounts a white steed, and distributes sweets to passersby on his ride to Dam Square, assisted by a covey of young helpers. The infamous, week-long **Cannabis Cup Awards** festival, hosted annually by *High Times* magazine, celebrates marijuana and awards prizes for the best of the weed lot. Includes a Hemp Expo. Third week of the month.

December: **St. Nicholas Day** on the 5th is celebrated much as Christmas Day is in other countries: the city's shops and restaurants close early and Amsterdammers stay home to exchange gifts, seasonal sweets, and poetry (yes, verse lives—isn't it great?). Each year a Dfl 10,000 purse is awarded to the best entry at the **International Documentary Filmfestival Amsterdam** (tel 020/627–3329).

Gay and lesbian resources... Amsterdam is one of the most gay-friendly cities in Europe. The four gayest areas of town are **Warmoesstraat** (abuts the Red Light District, heavy leather, very butch); **along the Amstel** (yuppie gay couples sip beer in riverside cafes after a night at the ballet); **Reguliersdwarsstraat** (one of the city's most popular club streets for both gays and straights); and on **Kerkstraat** (site of raucous gay street parties). Gay prostitutes are known to troll **Nieuwe Zijds Voorburgwal** and **Spuistraat** at midnight and into the wee hours. The **Gay and Lesbian Switchboard** (tel 020/ 623–6565, until 10pm daily) has English speakers who dispense advice, directions, and advice about gay-friendly clubs, bookstores, hotels, cafes, and events. Available in bookstores, the **"Gay Tourist Map"** lists about two dozen gay hotels, and the *Best Guide to Amsterdam & the Benelux* is a top-notch guide to the city's gay scene for both men and women. If you can muddle through the Dutch, *De Gay Krant*, a biweekly newspaper published and available in gay clubs and bookstores, will help you map out your own lavender tour of the city. The bulletin board and staff at **Vrouwenhuis** (tel 020/625–2066; Nieuwe Herengracht 95, open until 11pm) are tapped into happenings for lesbians. The gay and lesbian book-store **Vrolijk** (tel 020/623–5142; Paleisstraat 135, open until 7 pm Mon–Wed and Fri–Sat, until 9 on Thur) stocks English books, magazines, and stacks of leaflets about gay and lesbian clubs, parties, seminars, and events.

Holidays... Expect banks, restaurants, shops, and cafes to be closed on Jan 1 (New Year's Day); Good Friday, Easter, and Easter Monday; Apr 30 (Queen's Day); Ascension Day (40 days after Easter); Pentecost (the seventh Sunday after Easter); May 5 (Liberation Day); Dec 5 (St. Nicholas Day); Dec 25 and 26 (Christmas).

Money matters... Most exchange offices (*buereaux de change*) and banks close well before nighttime. Bank hours are 9–4 on weekdays. The branch of **GWK** (Grens Wissel Kantoor) in the Centraal Station and the one in Schipol Airport are open 24 hours a day and usually offer exchange rates on par with the banks. Other GWK branches with nighttime hours are at Damrak 86 (open until 11:45pm) and Leidseplein 123 (open until midnight). GWK also gives cash advances on all major credit cards and sells *strip-penkaart* tickets for buses, trams, and the Metro. Avoid the sleazy *bureaux de change* on Damrak and Leidsestraat and other touristy areas; they charge high commissions. Automatic teller machines (ATMs) in Amsterdam are useful only for cash draws against major credit cards. Most accept the big plastic names—AmEx, MasterCard, Diner's Club—but won't take Visa. Go figure. A few branches of VSB Bank have bank machines that accept Visa: Singel 548, Haarlemmerdijk 177, Ceintuurbaan 95, and Van Baerlestraat 25 (all are open 24 hours).

Newspapers... No English-language daily is printed in Amsterdam. Bigger British and U.S. papers (*Wall Street Journal, USA Today*, and the *International Herald Tribune*) are readily available. Local daily papers are *Het Parool*, liberal afternoon paper; **De Volkskrant**, a liberal, Catholic morning paper; *De Telegraaf*, a reactionary rag; and *NRC Handelsblad*, middle-of-the-road evening paper for the intelligentsia.

Online information... To find information about Amsterdam on the World Wide Web, try http://www. euro.snickers.com/Travel/Routh/ams.html or http:// www.euro.net/5thworth/coffee/coffee.html. An e-mail address for travel information is: dtt@infotree.nl; keywords: Holland homepage. (See The Bar and Cafe Scene chapters for a listing of online cafes plugged into the Internet.)

Parking... The people at the VVV will tell you not to drive in Amsterdam. Every guidebook ever written about the city in any language says don't drive in Amsterdam. Everyone who has ever been to Amsterdam will tell you not to drive in Amsterdam. Just say no. But if you're a rebel and this is your misguided cause, good luck. Park anywhere signs will allow; they're understandable even to non-Dutch speakers.

Public transportation... The good news is that Amsterdam has an easy, affordable, and efficient system of trams, buses, and trains (subway and intercity). The **GVB** office just outside Centraal Station has everything you'll need: English-speaking assistance, maps, and *strippenkaart* (a cardboard sheet with 15 boxes or strips that each cover one zone. The city center, which encompasses 99 percent of the tourist sites, is in one zone. With each ride on a bus, tram, or Metro, you leave one strip blank and stamp the following strip in machines at all public transportation. More than one person can ride on one *strippenkaart*, if there are enough unused strips). The bad news about the city's various fleets is that most of the lines stop running at midnight. For motorized assistance after the witching hour, look for the special night buses, which run between midnight and 2am—they're all numbered in the 70s (for the numerically impaired). After 2, it's a taxi or your feet.

Radio... **Radio 100** (98.2 FM), a pirate radio station that favors world music; **Radio Patapoe** (101.5 FM), a commercial-free pirate station with the sort of diverse musical programming found on college radio stations; **BBC World Service** (648 AM) with news in English every hour on the hour; **MVS** (106.8 FM), a gay-operated station with interviews and news in English on Sundays from 6-8pm; **Radio de Frije Keyser** (96.2 FM), another pirate station with politics interspersed with music and occasional English-speaking deejays; **World Radio Network** (97 FM) with news from worldwide radio stations, most in English; and **Voice of America for Europe** (99.1 FM), music and propaganda for US troops abroad.

Taxis... Don't expect to find a lot of empty cabs cruising the streets of Amsterdam; most of the drivers prefer to wait at the city's taxi stands. You'll have the best luck flagging one down on the busy streets where people roam in packs: **Damrak**, **Amstelstraat**, **Leidsestraat**, **Raadhuisstraat**, **Rokin**. The biggest taxi stands are at Dam Square, Centraal Station, Spui, Westermarkt, Leidseplein, and Rembrandtplein. The central dispatch station for all city cabs is **Blokband Taxi** (tel 020/677–7777, 24 hours daily). Taxis are metered and begin at Dfl 5.60; each subsequent kilometer is Dfl 2.80, and bags ride for free. Taxis will take up to six passengers. It's customary to tip cab drivers about 10 percent of the fare. You should have no trouble communicating with your driver, since taxi drivers must be able to speak English to secure a license.

Tickets... The official sources for information and tickets are the **VVV,** the city's hyper-efficient tourist bureau (see Visitor Information, below) and the **AUB Uitboro,** a government-funded, cultural clearinghouse (see Events Information, above). Both offices distribute reams of information and sell tickets to almost everything happening in town, including films. Another option is to make your own reservations at the venue box office. Unlike other large cities with a thriving cultural scene, there are no back-door agencies, half-price wholesalers, or known nefarious means of procuring tickets on the sly. Tickets for major rock concerts are also for sale at **Nieuwe Muziek Handel** (tel 020/623–7321; Leidsestraat 50, open until 6pm). For B-team bands appearing at clubs, buy tickets at the door the night of the show. Keep in mind that credit cards are generally **not** accepted for tickets. Major classical events in opera, ballet, dance, and theater are likely to be sold out weeks in advance. To book tickets in advance from the U.S., call the VVV, the AUB, or the **National Reservations Center** (tel 070/317–5454, fax 070/320–2611; P.O. Box 404, 2260 AK Leidschendam, Netherlands), a reservations center for lodging that will also book tickets for major events. And if an event is sold out, don't count on hoisting a hand-lettered sign outside the venue and waiting for scalpers. It's just not done here.

Time... Amsterdam is six hours ahead of Eastern Standard Time, nine ahead of Pacific Time.

Visitor information... The VVV (pronounced "vay, vay, vay"), the country's official tourist board, has three branches in Amsterdam. (The initials stand for *Vereniging Voor Vreemdelingenverkeer,* which translates into the rather "X-File"-ish phrase, "Association for Alien Traffic.") The board and its multilingual staff are a model of efficiency and professionalism. For a small fee (which must pay for their patience) the office provides one-stop aid for travelers: it books hotel rooms, sells tickets to entertainment events, conducts tours, and distributes maps, informational brochures, and leaflets. It costs 75 cents a minute to access their main information number (tel 063/403–4066, 9–5 daily), and the meter runs quickly. It's best to visit in person and jam all their giveaway brochures into your backpack: Stationsplein 10 (in front of Centraal Station, 9–5 daily); Leidesplein 1 (9–7 daily); and farther-flung but uncrowded Stadionplein 10 (Van Tuyll Van, Serooskerkenweg 125, 9–5 daily). For correspondence: 901, 1001 AS Amsterdam. The **Netherlands Board of Tourism** (NTB) has U.S. offices at 355 Lexington Ave., New York, NY 10017, tel 212/246–1429, fax 212/333–3603; 225 N. Michigan Ave., Suite 326, Chicago, IL 60601, tel 312/819–0300, fax 312/819–1740; and 9841 Airport Blvd., Los Angeles, CA 90045, tel 310/348–9339, fax 310/348–9344. NBT Canada: 25 Adelaide St. E., Suite 710, Toronto, ON M5C 1Y2, tel 416/363–1577, fax 416/363–1577.

Weather... Not one of the city's main draws. Winters can be brutally cold with winds, ice, and bone-jarring dampness (but hey, the ice skating is fabulous). Spring brings rain and more dampness. Summer's alleged warm weather is brief, usually making an appearance in July and August, with humidity and mosquitos that spread like wildfire on the canals. Always pack a jacket and an umbrella, no matter what time of year.

Now Save Money On All Your Travels By Joining
FROMMER'S™ TRAVEL BOOK CLUB
The World's Best Travel Guides
At Membership Prices!

Frommer's Travel Book Club is your ticket to successful travel! Open up a world of travel information and simplify your travel planning when you join ranks with thousands of value-conscious travelers who are members of the Frommer's *Travel Book Club*. Join today and you'll be entitled to all the privileges that come from belonging to the club that offers you travel guides for less to more than 100 destinations worldwide. **Annual membership is only $25.00 (U.S.) or $35.00 (Canada/Foreign).**

The Advantages of Membership:

1. Your choice of **three free** books (any **two** Frommer's Comprehensive Guides, Frommer's $-A-Day Guides, Frommer's Walking Tours or Frommer's Family Guides—plus **one** Frommer's City Guide, Frommer's City $-A-Day Guide or Frommer's Touring Guide).

2. Your own subscription to the **TRIPS & TRAVEL** quarterly newsletter.

3. You're entitled to a **30% discount** on your order of any additional books offered by the club.

4. You're offered (at a small additional fee) our **Domestic Trip-Routing Kits.**

Our **Trips & Travel** quarterly newsletter offers practical information on the best buys in travel, the "hottest" vacation spots, the latest travel trends, world-class events and much, much more.

Our **Domestic Trip-Routing Kits** are available for any North American destination. We'll send you a detailed map highlighting the best route to take to your destination—you can request direct or scenic routes.

Here's all you have to do to join:

Send in your membership fee of $25.00 ($35.00 Canada/Foreign) with your name and address on the form below along with your selections as part of your membership package to the address listed below. Remember to check off your three free books.

If you would like to order additional books, please select the books you would like and send a check for the total amount (please add sales tax in the states noted below), plus $2.00 per book for shipping and handling ($3.00 Canada/Foreign) to the address listed below.

FROMMER'S TRAVEL BOOK CLUB
P.O. Box 473
Mt. Morris, IL 61054-0473
(815) 734-1104

[ ] **YES!** I want to take advantage of this opportunity to join Frommer's Travel Book Club.

[ ] My check is enclosed. Dollar amount enclosed_____*
(all payments in U.S. funds only)

Name _____

Address _____

City _____ State _____ Zip _____

Phone ( ) _____(In case we have a question regarding your order).

All orders must be prepaid.

To ensure that all orders are processed efficiently, please apply sales tax in the following areas: CA, CT, FL, IL, IN, NJ, NY, PA, TN, WA and CANADA.

*With membership, shipping & handling will be paid by Frommer's Travel Book Club for the three FREE books you select as part of your membership. Please add $2.00 per book for shipping & handling for any additional books purchased ($3.00 Canada/Foreign).

Allow 4-6 weeks for delivery for all items. Prices of books, membership fee, and publication dates are subject to change without notice. All orders are subject to acceptance and availability.

Please send me the books checked below:

FROMMER'S COMPREHENSIVE GUIDES

*(Guides listing facilities from budget to deluxe,
with emphasis on the medium-priced)*

	Retail Price	Code		Retail Price	Code
☐ Acapulco/Ixtapa/Taxco, 2nd Edition	$13.95	C157	☐ Jamaica/Barbados, 2nd Edition	$15.00	C149
☐ Alaska '94-'95	$17.00	C131	☐ Japan '94-'95	$19.00	C144
☐ Arizona '95 (Avail. 3/95)	$14.95	C166	☐ Maui, 1st Edition	$14.00	C153
☐ Australia '94'-'95	$18.00	C147	☐ Nepal, 2nd Edition	$18.00	C126
☐ Austria, 6th Edition	$16.95	C162	☐ New England '95	$16.95	C165
☐ Bahamas '94-'95	$17.00	C121	☐ New Mexico, 3rd Edition (Avail. 3/95)	$14.95	C167
☐ Belgium/Holland/ Luxembourg '93-'94	$18.00	C106	☐ New York State '94-'95	$19.00	C133
☐ Bermuda '94-'95	$15.00	C122	☐ Northwest, 5th Edition	$17.00	C140
☐ Brazil, 3rd Edition	$20.00	C111	☐ Portugal '94-'95	$17.00	C141
☐ California '95	$16.95	C164	☐ Puerto Rico '95-'96	$14.00	C151
☐ Canada '94-'95	$19.00	C145	☐ Puerto Vallarta/ Manzanillo/Guadalajara '94-'95	$14.00	C135
☐ Caribbean '95	$18.00	C148			
☐ Carolinas/Georgia, 2nd Edition	$17.00	C128	☐ Scandinavia, 16th Edition (Avail. 3/95)	$19.95	C169
☐ Colorado, 2nd Edition	$16.00	C143	☐ Scotland '94-'95	$17.00	C146
☐ Costa Rica '95	$13.95	C161	☐ South Pacific '94-'95	$20.00	C138
☐ Cruises '95-'96	$19.00	C150	☐ Spain, 16th Edition	$16.95	C163
☐ Delaware/Maryland '94-'95	$15.00	C136	☐ Switzerland/ Liechtenstein '94-'95	$19.00	C139
☐ England '95	$17.95	C159	☐ Thailand, 2nd Edition	$17.95	C154
☐ Florida '95	$18.00	C152	☐ U.S.A., 4th Edition	$18.95	C156
☐ France '94-'95	$20.00	C132	☐ Virgin Islands '94-'95	$13.00	C127
☐ Germany '95	$18.95	C158	☐ Virginia '94-'95	$14.00	C142
☐ Ireland, 1st Edition (Avail. 3/95)	$16.95	C168	☐ Yucatan, 2nd Edition	$13.95	C155
☐ Italy '95	$18.95	C160			

FROMMER'S $-A-DAY GUIDES

(Guides to low-cost tourist accommodations and facilities)

	Retail Price	Code		Retail Price	Code
☐ Australia on $45 '95-'96	$18.00	D122	☐ Israel on $45, 15th Edition	$16.95	D130
☐ Costa Rica/Guatemala/ Belize on $35, 3rd Edition	$15.95	D126	☐ Mexico on $45 '95	$16.95	D125
			☐ New York on $70 '94-'95	$16.00	D121
☐ Eastern Europe on $30, 5th Edition	$16.95	D129	☐ New Zealand on $45 '93-'94	$18.00	D103
☐ England on $60 '95	$17.95	D128			
☐ Europe on $50 '95	$17.95	D127	☐ South America on $40, 16th Edition	$18.95	D123
☐ Greece on $45 '93-'94	$19.00	D100			
☐ Hawaii on $75 '95	$16.95	D124	☐ Washington, D.C. on $50 '94-'95	$17.00	D120
☐ Ireland on $45 '94-'95	$17.00	D118			

FROMMER'S CITY $-A-DAY GUIDES

	Retail Price	Code		Retail Price	Code
☐ Berlin on $40 '94-'95	$12.00	D111	☐ Madrid on $50 '94-'95	$13.00	D119
☐ London on $45 '94-'95	$12.00	D114	☐ Paris on $50 '94-'95	$12.00	D117

FROMMER'S FAMILY GUIDES

*(Guides listing information on kid-friendly
hotels, restaurants, activities and attractions)*

	Retail Price	Code		Retail Price	Code
☐ California with Kids	$18.00	F100	☐ San Francisco with Kids	$17.00	F104
☐ Los Angeles with Kids	$17.00	F103	☐ Washington, D.C.		
☐ New York City			with Kids	$17.00	F102
with Kids	$18.00	F101			

FROMMER'S CITY GUIDES

*(Pocket-size guides to sightseeing and tourist
accommodations and facilities in all price ranges)*

	Retail Price	Code		Retail Price	Code
☐ Amsterdam '93-'94	$13.00	S110	☐ Montreal/Quebec City '95	$11.95	S166
☐ Athens, 10th Edition			☐ Nashville/Memphis,		
(Avail. 3/95)	$12.95	S174	1st Edition	$13.00	S141
☐ Atlanta '95	$12.95	S161	☐ New Orleans '95	$12.95	S148
☐ Atlantic City/Cape May,			☐ New York '95	$12.95	S152
5th Edition	$13.00	S130	☐ Orlando '95	$13.00	S145
☐ Bangkok, 2nd Edition	$12.95	S147	☐ Paris '95	$12.95	S150
☐ Barcelona '93-'94	$13.00	S115	☐ Philadelphia, 8th Edition	$12.95	S167
☐ Berlin, 3rd Edition	$12.95	S162	☐ Prague '94-'95	$13.00	S143
☐ Boston '95	$12.95	S160	☐ Rome, 10th Edition	$12.95	S168
☐ Budapest, 1st Edition	$13.00	S139	☐ St. Louis/Kansas City,		
☐ Chicago '95	$12.95	S169	2nd Edition	$13.00	S127
☐ Denver/Boulder/Colorado			☐ San Diego '95	$12.95	S158
Springs, 3rd Edition	$12.95	S154	☐ San Francisco '95	$12.95	S155
☐ Dublin, 2nd Edition	$12.95	S157	☐ Santa Fe/Taos/		
☐ Hong Kong '94-'95	$13.00	S140	Albuquerque '95		
☐ Honolulu/Oahu '95	$12.95	S151	(Avail. 2/95)	$12.95	S172
☐ Las Vegas '95	$12.95	S163	☐ Seattle/Portland '94-'95	$13.00	S137
☐ London '95	$12.95	S156	☐ Sydney, 4th Edition	$12.95	S171
☐ Los Angeles '95	$12.95	S164	☐ Tampa/St. Petersburg,		
☐ Madrid/Costa del Sol,			3rd Edition	$13.00	S146
2nd Edition	$12.95	S165	☐ Tokyo '94-'95	$13.00	S144
☐ Mexico City, 1st Edition	$12.95	S170	☐ Toronto '95 (Avail. 3/95)	$12.95	S173
☐ Miami '95-'96	$12.95	S149	☐ Vancouver/Victoria '94-'95	$13.00	S142
☐ Minneapolis/St. Paul,			☐ Washington, D.C. '95	$12.95	S153
4th Edition	$12.95	S159			

FROMMER'S WALKING TOURS

*(Companion guides that point out the places
and pleasures that make a city unique)*

	Retail Price	Code		Retail Price	Code
☐ Berlin	$12.00	W100	☐ New York	$12.00	W102
☐ Chicago	$12.00	W107	☐ Paris	$12.00	W103
☐ England's Favorite Cities	$12.00	W108	☐ San Francisco	$12.00	W104
☐ London	$12.00	W101	☐ Washington, D.C.	$12.00	W105
☐ Montreal/Quebec City	$12.00	W106			

SPECIAL EDITIONS

	Retail Price	Code		Retail Price	Code
☐ Bed & Breakfast Southwest	$16.00	P100	☐ National Park Guide, 29th Edition	$17.00	P106
☐ Bed & Breakfast Great American Cities	$16.00	P104	☐ Where to Stay U.S.A., 11th Edition	$15.00	P102
☐ Caribbean Hideaways	$16.00	P103			

FROMMER'S TOURING GUIDES

*(Color-illustrated guides that include walking tours,
cultural and historic sites, and practical information)*

	Retail Price	Code		Retail Price	Code
☐ Amsterdam	$11.00	T001	☐ New York	$11.00	T008
☐ Barcelona	$14.00	T015	☐ Rome	$11.00	T010
☐ Brazil	$11.00	T003	☐ Tokyo	$15.00	T016
☐ Hong Kong/Singapore/ Macau	$11.00	T006	☐ Turkey	$11.00	T013
☐ London	$13.00	T007	☐ Venice	$ 9.00	T014

*Please note: If the availability of a book is several months away, we may
have back issues of guides to that particular destination.
Call customer service at (815) 734-1104.*